The Marriage of Heaven and Earth — a Visual Guide to N.T. Wright

50 pictures to explain the rock star theologian of our day

By Marlin Watling

Published by Marlin Watling:
69207 Sandhausen, Germany
marlin@mosaikhd.de

Cover design by Constanze von der Goltz and Motoki Tonn, Lumen Design
Illustration concepts by Marlin Watling
Illustration artwork by Katja Tonn
Editing by Sandra Judd

What others are saying

"This is a very clever and useful introduction into the encyclopedic mind of the most prolific New Testament scholars of our generation. Tom Wright's thinking is a gift to those of us who seek to further understand the church in mission, discipleship in the way of Jesus, and life in the Kingdom of God. Marlin's book is a needed distillation of his key ideas. A good read."
- *Alan Hirsch, Author, Thought Leader, Activist, alanhirsch.org*

"The Lord Jesus had the amazing ability to make the complex simple - not simplistic but simple - and that meant that all who heard him could learn, remember and share his teaching. In this book Marlin Watling reveals the same facility - received from Jesus himself - to interpret the theological reflection of one of the world's greatest theologians, NT Wright. Now, Tom Wright's work can be read and understood by us all. And that is a great gift to every student of theology, Christian minister and interested lay man and woman."
- *Mike Breen, Founder of 3DM Movements*

"Marlin Watling captures complex ideas in cheeky drawings that are counter-intuitive and, frankly, dazzling. In this book, he takes some of the most epic propositions of contemporary biblical scholarship, all from the pen of N T Wright, and makes them accessible for us all. The result is convincing, enlightening and educational: it is impossible to read this book and not be better informed of the shape of N T Wright's thinking."
– Gerard Kelly, Director of The Bless Network and author of *The Seven Stories that Shape Your Life*

"*The Marriage of Heaven and Earth* is a very valuable summary of N.T. Wright's books put in a very readable and easy to understand format. I recommend this to any one as a helpful guide to a variety of important themes in scripture. I had read a few of N.T. Wright's books but after reading this summary by Marlin, I bought a larger set. Great book."
-Barry Wissler, President, HarvestNet International

"Sometimes we hear the phrase 'Seeing is believing'. In this brief but delightful book I think of the phrase 'Now I see that...' as if someone finally understands

words spoken or written. Marlin Watling provides wonderful visual echoes helping people 'see' the sometimes complex explanations of Prof. N.T. Wright. Tom Wright does not try to write in a complex style but the world and God's ways are intricately woven, requiring profound thinking, pondering, and explanation. Marlin has provided a very good guide to Tom Wright's basic lines of thinking about the world, the Bible, and about God's ways of working out the reconciling of all things to himself."
-David P. Seemuth, Ph.D., N.T. Wright Online

"What an amazing distillation of NT Wright's spiritual insights in a very readable format. Watling uses pictograms to help all of us, especially the rising generation, grasp these deep spiritual truths as expounded on by Wright in his many books. Use this simple and yet comprehensive primer for Bible studies, small group discussion and discipleship groups."
- Keith Blank, Bishop in Lancaster Mennonite Conference, Lancaster, PA

Table of Contents

Prologue

Image runs the world.

Turn on your computer and go to today's hottest websites—Facebook, Pinterest, Youtube, Twitter, Instagram. These are sites driven by images and short comments that allow you to share and connect with others. It is a sign of our time that information is condensed, and the image rules over the long thoughts of conceptual pieces. The popular mind is busy and sifts through loads of input in any single day.

And then come we Christians. With our sermons, with our opinions, with our arguments. While some churches dig in to the image-driven style, we do find it a challenge to connect our thoughts to the larger culture. Which is a pity. The culture is so fragmented that people are looking for orientation. A larger story is sorely lacking from our society. And so companies try to infuse "purpose statements" into their factories, and nonprofits focus on selling their "mission" to save some aspect of the planet. Coaching hits an all-time high. Being at the "right place, at the right time" hits an all-time low. Wouldn't it be nice if the Greatest Story Ever Told would provide that sense of destiny that people so obviously need? Wouldn't it be great if the Gospel would give people that deep sense of purpose, of location, of motion that everyone seeks?

How about we try some images? Since this is the language of our day, we could try to refocus on what we are actually saying. It turns out, though, that most of what we have been saying is wrong. That is, at least according to NT Wright. The bishop, professor, writer, and Christian is one of today's most prominent voices. He writes faster than Michael Jordan scored on his best days. And in his writing he has covered the vast spectrum of Christian thought: liturgy and virtue, church and missions, devotions and theology, history and how we know things. He writes under two brands: as NT Wright for the academic world, with the sweeping six-book series on *Christian Origins and the Question of God*, and as Tom Wright for the more popular audience, with topics including character, worship, resurrection, the Gospel, Jesus, the Kingdom of God, the Bible, and probably one hundred other things.

So what does the most prominent theologian of our day have to say to us? We have read all of his works and decided they are worth a compact summary. NT Wright is on to something. Something big. Something that changes everything. Literally. So, we took his most popular works and drew images. Little sketches that explain his key ideas. And once we were done, we picked the best and reordered them to explain the core of his thoughts. A picture speaks more than a thousand words. With the following images you will get an introduction to the big picture of the Bible and its implications for our time. You will get NT Wright in a few hours (a feat seemed impossible until now). You will get images that connect your story to the larger story of the world. You will be called into your life's mission.

The book is broken up into four parts. Part one introduces you to Tom and his life. Part two shows you what he brings fresh to the table—his unique insights that shake the church. We have focused on four in particular: how to read the Bible as a story, including the Torah-bit that covers the Old Testament; how the events of Jesus' life shape our grasp of the Gospel; a new understanding of the kingdom of God as God's new creation started here; and finally how to understand morals without moralizing or a condescending attitude.

Part three then moves to some of the implications of this changed story: the renewal of the mind, how to live as God's image in our time, and how to confront evil in our world. Part four talks about what it means to live in God's new world—what the hope is going forward, what life after death means, and why our work is not in vain.

Along the way we dive into three major theological ideas, as well as correct some of the key theories that modern Christianity got wrong: how to read the Bible, how to spell out the Good News, how to deal with morals, and what to hope for. Heavy stuff, with all sorts of potential to rough up some long-settled misunderstandings.

We are indebted to NT Wright first, of course. All the ideas here originate from him, and we take on the role of "translator": from the world of paragraphs to those of images. We have informed him about our work and he seemed happy, but did not have the time to get involved or quality-check us. Free speech instead.

A number of people have provided valuable feedback on the drafts – Prof. David Seemuth (who runs ntwrightonline and offers online courses with NT Wright), Derek Vreeland, Ed Einsiedler, Cris Zimmermann, Gerard Kelly, Christian Lessing, Philip Zimmermann and Barry Wissler. Katja Tonn has brought the illustrations to a professional standard, Constanze von der Golz designed the cover, and Motoki Tonn oversaw the art direction.

Our language teacher has been Dan Roam, whose back-of-the-napkin style has been the trigger for this series. His toolkit is valuable and should grow in importance.

Finally, our local churches and our very own network (Spark Europe) have provided a context to discuss, reflect on, and implement a lot of these ideas.

With that, welcome to Tom's world…

Marlin Watling
Heidelberg, August 2016

Part One. NT Wright, Rock Star of Theology

This is Tom

Nicholas Thomas Wright, the guy this book covers

THIS is Tom. He is doing to our time what Martin Luther did to his: changing our view of God. And opening up a new vista on life and the character of God.

Tom was born on December 1, 1948, in the northernmost corner of England, and his full name is Nicholas Thomas Wright. This is why he is often called "NT Wright." Since he is very personable, he prefers to go by "Tom" and writes under that name in his more popular books. He has been married to his wife Maggie for over forty years, and he has two sons and two daughters. He enjoys music, hiking, and golf and supports the Newcastle United Football Club.

His career

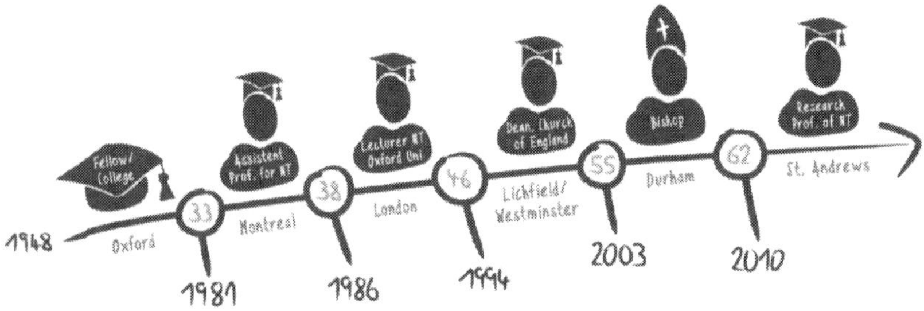

Scholarship meets church life

Tom has spent most of his time in England. In school he focused on the "classics," then spent three years at Exeter College in Oxford studying classic literature. As you can tell, he likes stories and older times. In 1971, he added two years of theology to the mix and graduated with a BA in theology. He studied another four years at Oxford in Anglican ministry and finished with an MA and doctorate of divinity degree. At the age of twenty-seven, he was ready to hit the world, and he…

Studied some more. For the next six years he stayed at Oxford, researching and working on his PhD. His main question was Romans. The title of his 355-page thesis was "*The Messiah and the People of God: A Study in Pauline Theology with Particular Reference to the Argument of the Epistle to the Romans.*"

At thirty-three, he became an assistant professor in Montreal, Canada—his only stint outside of his home country. The area he taught on was the New

Testament. He continued teaching and tutoring the New Testament in Montreal for five years, and then later back in the United Kingdom for another seven years.

In 1994, he moved to a parish role, first at a local church, and then later moving on to become a bishop. The Bishop of Durham is a much esteemed position in the Anglican Church, and Tom held this position for seven years. After sixteen years as a pastor, he went back to academics in 2010 as the Research Professor of New Testament and Early Christianity at St Mary's College, St Andrews in Scotland.

He had a long career on many fronts. This is what Tom had to say in a talk at Regent College in 1992:

I still often do not know whether I do belong in the church or whether I do belong in the academy. Because I am trying to be both and I am called to be both. ... I have done my best to preach and pray as a serious historian; and do my historical work as a serious preacher and prayer. Result: some fellow historians call me a fundamentalist; some fellow believers call me a compromised pseudo-liberal.

In my experience it has been precisely when I found myself—often unwillingly—in prayer at one of those fault lines that I have known not just the presence and comfort of the living Messiah, but have discovered that the one with whom I was wrestling and who has left me limping was the angel of the Lord. I have been reassured again and again that my calling is not to solve the great dualists of our post-enlightenment and post-modern world but to live in prayer where the world is in pain in my own discipline. In assurance that through these means, in a level far deeper than the articulate solving of the problems, my discipline will find new fruitfulness and my church perhaps new directions. Out of that may grow, I pray, work that is peacemaking and fruitful. The darkest times have often been the most productive, at every level.[1]

His works

Tom fills many libraries—he published in three main areas

TOM has been a busy writer. There are dozens of popular and academic books under his name, along with articles, chapters, conference appearances, and interviews. He borders on fifty books published to date. Someone called him "very media-friendly," as he talks to many people who ask. YouTube shows many eloquent presentations by Tom on various topics.

Tom's academic career focuses mainly on the theology of the New Testament, with a major on Paul as well as historic interest. His big series is called "Christian Origins and the Question of God" and will be six volumes long. "Long" is the key word here. Each of the volumes is more than 500 pages, with volume 4 (*Paul and the Faithfulness of God*) being more than 1,700 pages long.

Tom also wrote a commentary series on the New Testament. The "For everyone" series covers all of the books of the New Testament. In eighteen volumes and more than four thousand he breaks down each segment of the New Testament and writes an explanation of what is going on in that segment. With both a historical perspective and a devotional target, it is easy reading and vast in scope.

Then there are his popular books. *Surprised by Hope* (published in 2008) might be the most well-known, followed by *Simply Christian* (2010) and *Simply Jesus* (2008). The topics cover Jesus, of course, then discipleship, character, life after death, evil, the psalms, justification, the Bible, and various aspects of philosophy.

Oh, and he translated the New Testament. His version is called *the Kingdom New Testament.*

What drives him

The driving force behind Tom Wright—what did the New Testament really mean to people in the first century?

TOM is driven by the quest to better understand the meaning of the message of Jesus. He digs into the times and expectations of the New Testament to get a clear view on this. His main academic books are titled "Christian Origins," and this shows that he is a historian by heart. He wants to understand Christianity's origins: what it meant when it started. What did Jesus intend? What significance did his life and actions have? How can history and theology come together?

These questions lie at the heart of Tom's work. And that is important. These questions are very different than most popular theological questions. Or most questions that sermons pick up.

Most churches address issues like how can I be saved? Or how can I have a relationship with God? (And sometimes even more practical, everyday-happiness kind of stuff). Martin Luther came up with big ideas once he started asking new questions, such as how a sinful man can stand before a just God. The breakthrough came when he followed that question.

As Tom followed his historical quest he came up with a different set of eyes with which to look at the Bible. Less about him and more about God. And more along the lines of "how is God going to run his world project?" Tom shared his ambition in an interview:

> *I would like to think that people would say, "He opened up the New Testament and showed us what was there all along. He enabled us to grasp it in a way that made sense rather than just a few verses here and there, and the rest is fuzzy."*[2]

Different questions, different answers, more insights. This is why we have this book. A new time of breakthrough is upon us. It changes how we see God. It changes how we see ourselves. It changes how we see the world. Some are catching on to this…

In the spotlight

Tom featured on the cover of some of the biggest magazines in our day.

ALL of this work has led to a bit of fame for Tom. Some people call him the "most influential theologian" of our time. Others call him the "rock star theologian of our generation" and compare him to C. S. Lewis, Karl Barth, or even Martin Luther. *Christianity Today* comments on Tom: "People who are asked to write about N. T. Wright may find they quickly run out of superlatives. He is the most prolific biblical scholar in a generation."[3]

In 2008 and 2012 he was featured in *Time Magazine*, one of the world's largest magazines. It is not often that such a prominent magazine asks the opinion of a theologian whose advice to young leaders is to "pray and read the Bible." They called him "one of the most formidable figures in the world of Christian thought." On both occasions, Tom was quoted extensively, and this is what the editor had to say:

> *If heaven is understood more as God's space on earth than as an ethereal region apart from the essential reality we know, then what happens on earth matters even more than we think, for the Christian life becomes a continuation of the unfolding work of Jesus, who will one day return to set the world to rights.*[4]

Big words written in a big magazine. Tom speaks in public places. This matches his belief that who Jesus is and what he did is more than a private matter. It changes everything. The life, death, and resurrection of Jesus is public truth

The Luther of our day: A true reformer

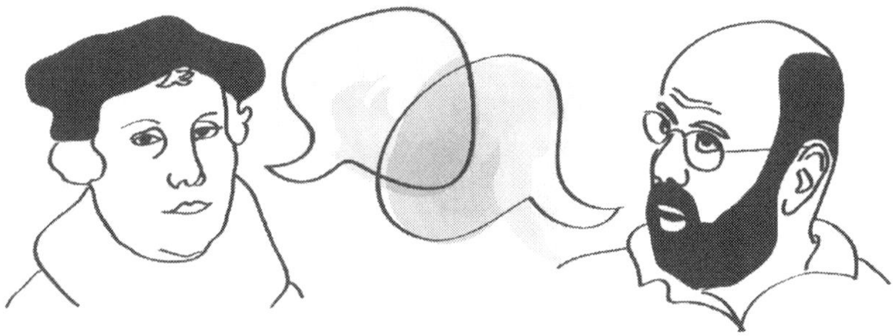

Martin Luther and Tom Wright—two true reformers

WHEN Martin Luther nailed his ninety-five statements to a door in Wittenberg, Germany, he shook the earth and changed church history. Luther read his Bible and looked at the church. Something didn't match. The church sold forgiveness of sins, conveniently filling its coffers with a buck or two.

In 1517, Luther questioned those practices. More than that, he challenged a worldview. The role of the church was the keeper of Truth, and most people could neither read nor understand Latin. Theology was a professional play.

Luther set out to change that. He asked people to go back to the Bible and see for themselves. He translated the Bible to enable just that. The result: a major shift in the course of Christianity.

Five hundred years later, our setting is vastly different. Everyone has access to Bibles; direct contact with God is encouraged widely. Yet if we read our Bibles and look at the church, do they match? No, thinks Tom.

If we look at today's sermons and key messages, they are vastly different from the Bible's pages. Our message of grace, justification, and Jesus as your best bet miss major parts of the storyline. What about Israel? What about the Kingdom? What about creation? And what about the covenant of God with his people and the Torah?

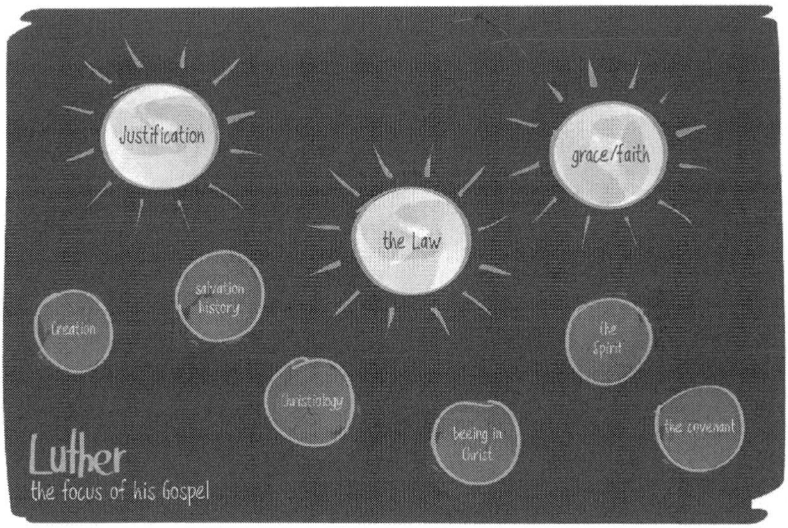

Luther highlighted a message of grace—and some important topics vanished in the background

If we look at Martin Luther's storyline, some issues run front and center. Basically, everything that is needed on how to be saved. Justification, the role of the law, grace, and faith. God and I get along now—that has far-reaching consequences on how to live life from there.

Look at the practice in churches today. Most struggle with serious discipleship. Missions are handled by a few, and morals become a reason for splitting relationships. Engaging with the burning issues of our day leaves us scrambling for words.

One of the main things I am here on earth to do is to study and teach the New Testament. And to bring as much of the study and teaching of the New Testament in the middle of the life of the church as I can ... as I've been pastoring, I became aware just how little of the Bible even so-called Bible-Christians actually understand.[5]

Time to reform again. Time to go back to the Great Book and look up what it really says. Not everyone will like it.

People often get upset when you teach them what is in the Bible rather than what they presume is in the Bible.

Every great reformer sheds light on something that was there but overlooked. Maybe it is time to put the story back together in a way that it was there all along, but never fully heard. Let's see what Tom opens up to us. Ready?

What is fresh in Tom

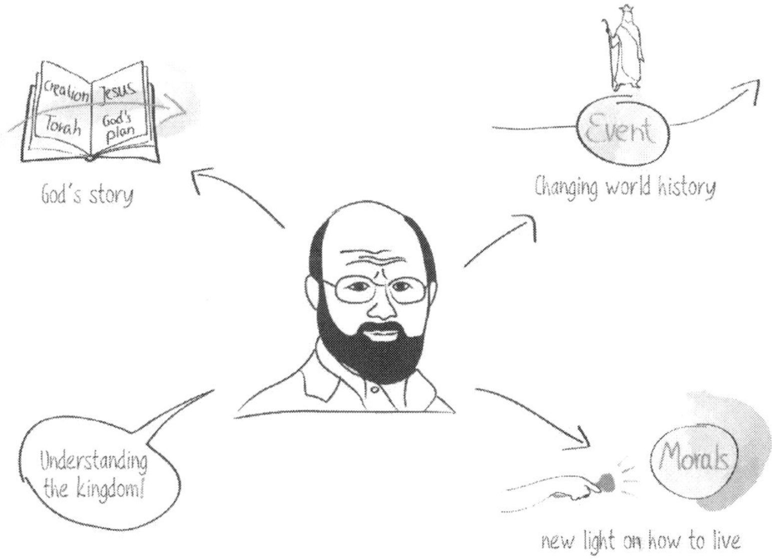

What is different? Tom reforms our understanding on four key pillars: the Gospel, Jesus' role in world history, the Kingdom of God, and morals.

THE other day, I was sitting with a group of young leaders in my living room and shared an overview of Tom's ideas. I gave them the Luther comparison and told them that we are seeing new things because of Tom. "So what exactly is new in Tom?" asked one of those present. "What is he saying that no one else says?"

It took me a minute to put into words what I had read over the years. So many good insights can be gained from any of Tom's books. Dealing with his brilliant mind can be overwhelming. He writes densely and thoroughly. In his thousands of pages we find recurring themes and ideas. Four key ideas stick out that he puts in a way that few other do. This changes the contours of our faith.

1. He connects the whole Bible and tells it as a story.

   Think about this for a second. The Old Testament runs over five hundred pages, and most people take away from it that "mankind is sinful" or "Israel and self-effort don't work." This seems like a lot of pages to share two simple ideas. There must be more, just as the apostles connected their presentation of Jesus with the story beforehand. Tom invites us back to understand the early parts of the story in more depth.

2. He puts the event back into Jesus (and redeems him from being an option).

   People these days accept faith as good, "if it helps you." For many, it is only one option among many for how to deal with life and find meaning. Even Christians are drawn into the faith by being shown the benefits: eternal life, forgiveness, meaning, and acceptance. The apostles had a different read on the story. While Jesus came with some of those benefits, the apostles talked about him as "Lord over all." They looked at him as the King of the world. The Gospel was News—something that happened and that changed everything. Tom rediscovers this world-changing claim and puts it at the center of the life of Jesus.

3. He sheds new light on the kingdom of God (it is new creation).

   The central message of Jesus was the kingdom of God. Yet, few people are able to explain it in easy terms. Most church confessions do not mention the term. How come? Tom unlocks the understanding of the kingdom as God's new creation that was started at the resurrection.

4. He unlocks a new take on morals.

   Christians have a hard time finding a voice in the public space on morals. It seems like some of the ideas are out of date, too uptight, or not connected enough to where people are. Yet, without morals we clearly lose the claim of Christianity to guide us how to live. Tom puts morals in the light of creation—being created in God's image and as God's stewards in the world. This angle invites us to consider life beyond right and wrong and asks us to live as redeemed people in a fallen world.

Four areas. Four key ideas. A whole new take on life, on God, on history.

Let's start with the most important of all guides—the Holy Book and how we deal with it.

Part Two. What Is New in Tom?

The Bible as story

We filter the story out of the mix

What we do to the Bible—take the story and try to distill something "timeless" out of it. Points and principles then replace the story and drama of Scripture.

THE other day, I watched a sermon on YouTube. A gifted preacher told the story of Jesus meeting Peter after the resurrection. Jesus told him to fish, and suddenly, the net burst. Then, Jesus had breakfast with the apostles and asked Peter how much he loved him. The takeaway? Three points.

Somehow, we see this all the time. Story gets translated to ideas. Drama boils down to principles. One wonders why Jesus didn't just tell us the principles. It almost seems like the Bible came along in the wrong format. Tom reminds us that the form of the Bible needs to inform our reading. Tom says about the shape of the Bible:

> *It is not, for a start, a list of rules, though it contains many commandments of various sorts and in various contexts. Nor is it a compendium of true doctrines, though of course many parts of the Bible declare great truths about God, Jesus, the world and ourselves in no uncertain terms. Most of its constituent parts, and all of it when put together can best be described as story. This is a complicated and much-discussed theme, but there is nothing to be gained by ignoring it.*[6]

The Holy Book is a story! Page 1 speaks to this: "In the beginning…". The event of Jesus comes along in story language: "when the time was fulfilled," "then he…," "it is finished…," and so on. Jesus acted and lived in a larger context, and he interacts with this context. You see parts in the light of the whole.

We often press the Bible through the filter of rational thinking and want to distill timeless principles. Rather than inviting people into the story of God, we want the principles to rule life. And in the process, sometimes we just hear our predispositions. We exchange the God story for God principles. We trade our Gospel into a quest for otherworldliness (what matters is stuff after life) or about inwardness (what matters is how it feels).

Can we approach the story of God as an unfolding development in which we are called to participate?

Understanding Scripture as a drama

This is the drama in 5 acts—the Bible tells a story leading up to something. We are now part of the age of the church, adding our part to the great storyline of history.

HOW, then, can we approach Scripture? The story demands that we start with the big overview and then fit the pieces into that frame. Tom offers a setup that provides this framework. Scripture starts with the perfect setup in creation and the Garden of Eden. Tom suggests that we look at Scripture like a five-act play. It starts with creation (Act 1): God expresses his goodness and creates humans for fellowship and as stewards over creation, reflecting his image. Then comes the fall (Act 2) and humans become alienated from God and each other. God elects Abraham and enters into covenant with Israel (Act 3) in order to have a people for himself who live in faithfulness to him. Jesus answers those expectations (Act 4) and starts God's new world in the middle of the present times. Now, we are living in the age of the church (Act 5) and working and waiting for the final consummation. Therefore, there will be more acts coming as heaven and earth interlock.

If we understand the major drama of the book, we are enabled to find our place in it and interpret what is going on. Like musicians who get to improvise in one part, we need to understand the drama and structure of what is going on before. Then we will be able to be both faithful and free to translate the drama to our times and our situations.

We know the final stage that we inhabit. It started at the day of Pentecost with the outpouring of the Spirit and the birth of the church. This is our place as move toward the conclusion. We live with the prayer of Jesus that, "your kingdom come and your will be done on earth as it is in heaven."

Why Abraham

This is how the Bible is set up. The good creation gets messed up. Then, God starts to sort out the sin of the world by calling Abraham. The start of the solution of the disjointed world is God's election of Abraham.

So many of us skip over the middle part, Act 3, the story of Israel. How come the Old Testament is such a long story? And is its only point that Israel is sinful and fleshly?

Tom gives us the gift of connecting the story better. Let's build on the five-act model. We start with God as the good Creator. He makes the world for his pleasure and to share with humans. This is Act 1. Then, humans go for independence. Act 2 ends in big problems. Relationships are screwed up, and distance grows. How is God going to deal with the world gone off-track? He needs to save the world somehow.

Let's pause for a second at this point. That question is actually super-important. Stories are driven by quests. The quest of the Bible narrative is exactly that: how does God save his world-project? (This is the question that differs so much from other questions like "how do we get to heaven?"— the answers and what we look for are vastly different.)

God's plan to save the world started with Abraham. In Genesis 12, we see God's start of a solution. The covenant with Abraham set in motion God's rescue operation for the world. The covenant pointed to a future—his promise of inheritance meant that the earth will be full with his heritage. Deuteronomy 27 spells out the covenant: obey God and you will be blessed and the world will see the light. Disobey God and you will be cursed, even to the point of being taken into exile.

> *The story that begins in Genesis 12 with God's call of Abraham has for its motto the promise, "In you all the families of the earth shall be blessed" (v. 3). This theme continues in one way or another in many parts of the Old Testament.*[7]

The rescue operation has started. The mess will be addressed.

And yet, the Abraham project did not fully succeed.

Striking a deal

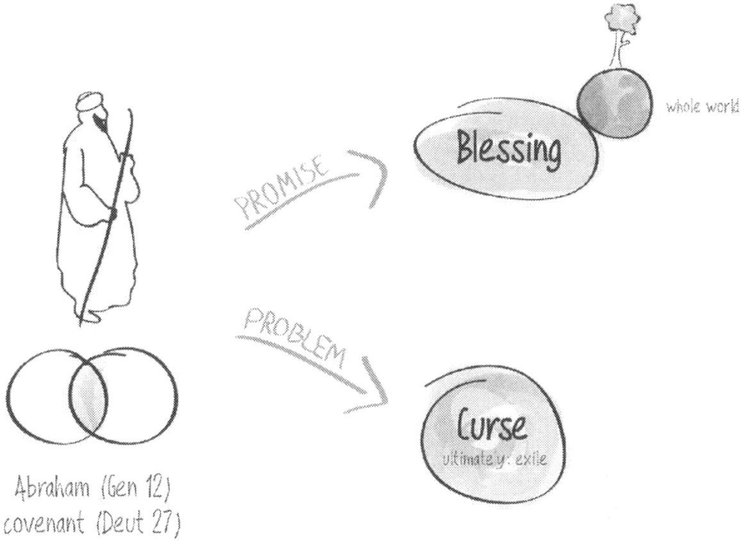

The Abraham project: call one man to contain evil and bless the world. If he acts on the promise, the whole world will be blessed. If he is unfaithful, a curse will come on his people.

God struck a covenant with Abraham. He elected him for a purpose. The deal was: God would be faithful to him and his offspring, and they would be his people. They were required to keep his commandments, mapped out in the Torah, and then would shine as a light to the world. If they were unfaithful, they would be cursed and ultimately taken into exile.

The original creation plan stayed in place: fill the earth with his glory. God put the calling and covenant in place to accomplish that.

Yet, Abraham and his offspring went for the lower option. They couldn't remain faithful. Sin was in their bones. They couldn't fulfill their purpose. They wandered into exile. How was God going to respond now?

The promise fulfilled

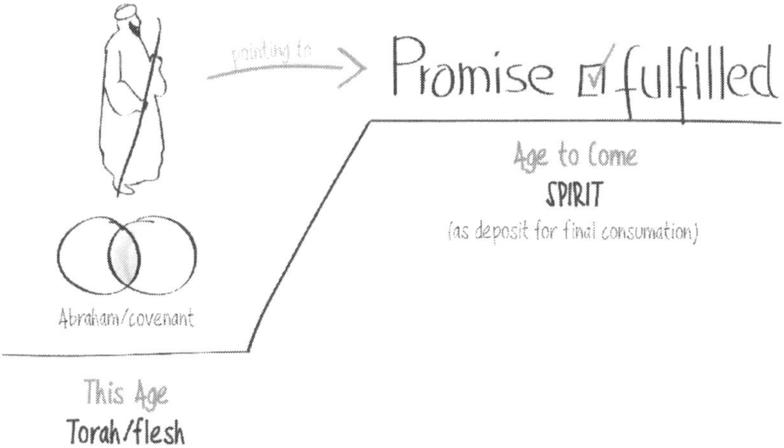

The Messiah ushers in the new age. Abraham represents promise and the time of Torah. In Jesus, the age of the Spirit came, the time of fulfillment. What was promised has now happened.

God responded by providing the solution. Jesus came on the scene and fulfilled the idea of the covenant. Yet somehow this took the Jews off guard. Sure, they were waiting for the "day of the Lord." They were aware that no number of moral bootstraps would put the world right. It was always a hope project.

Yet the utterly perplexing thing is that God did this within the old world. Everyone expected a complete overhaul. The key idea was "complete." Just solving the problem for some, and not dealing with the rest of the evil (like the Romans) was completely unacceptable for the Jews.

And yet the Bible claims exactly this: God acted. Jesus came as the servant figure that was foreshadowed in Isaiah. A human person who would take the fate of Israel on himself. God himself came to push the story forward. And he did so completely. Jesus hung on the cross and said, “It is finished.” We understand this only if we get the story leading to the cross. Tom has this to say about it:

> *We have tended in much modern Christianity to think of fulfillment as about way back then there were some prediction and prophecies and bits and types, and they all kind of leap over and land on Jesus. But there is no historic continuity between them. One of the points I really want is that we have to get used to seeing the Gospel as the story of Jesus bringing the story of Israel to its climax. It is this sense of continuity and of something radically new.*[8]

Messiah & Abraham

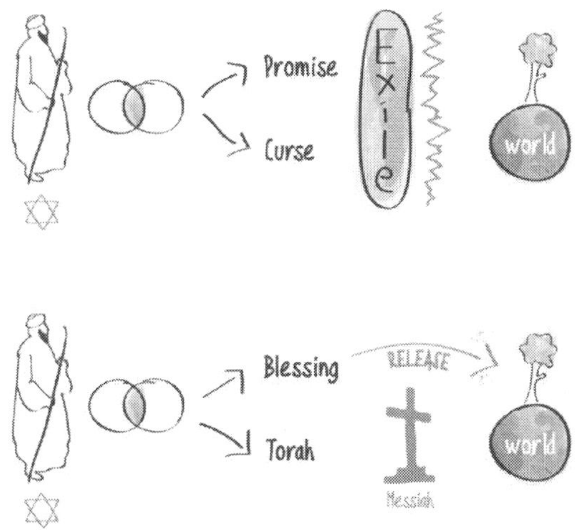

This is how Jesus connects to Abraham: Abraham was chosen to bring blessing to the world. He and his offspring were unfaithful to that call, so they ended up in exile and the blessing was blocked. Jesus fulfilled the call of Abraham and released the blessing to the world.

Jesus connects to Abraham and Israel. The quest is the same. How is God going to deal with the world? By dealing with the core problem in his way. Jesus came and on the cross exhausted sin and its power.

The story came full turn. Fulfillment. God had his way. Finally, the world was ready to be filled with him. Finally, the planet and the people were on track again. The quest was never to allow some to go to eternal bliss in some other dimension; it was always about dealing with what had gone wrong and setting it right.

And this is what we get by tracing the story through Abraham: the world made new. Yet to do it in stages was a complete surprise. To have God's kingdom in the middle of countries with taxes, with poor politicians, with blood, sweat, and tears—that still stuns people.

> *The world cannot cope with a Jesus who comes out of the tomb, who inaugurates God's new creation right in the middle of the old one.*[9]

This is big news! Surprising news. The message for our culture and our world speaks loud:

> *Perhaps the real challenge of Jesus's transformations within the material world is what they would imply both personally and politically. If they are about God becoming king on earth as in heaven, the chances are he's not going to stop with storms on lakes. There will be bigger fish to catch.*[10]

How will the story play out?

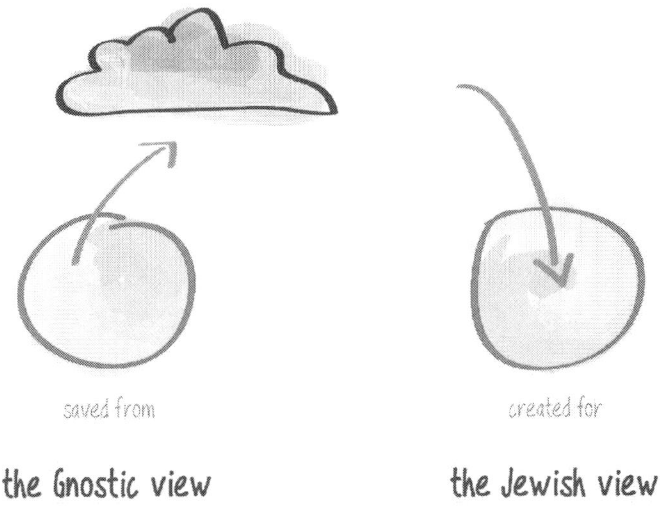

The Gnostics saw the world as bad, and so you were saved away from it. The Jewish view differs.

NOW we are ready to see the end of the drama more clearly. We can see how the story will play out. The quest of the Bible has been the setting right of God's intentions. In the Bible, we find a God who created. We see a God who is involved with his creation. We get to know a God who wants to flood the world with his love and care. We witness a God who redeems and renews.

Over the last centuries, we have started to think of heaven as an escape from this world. We have made the Gospel into a "spiritual agenda" and planned for some place other than this earth. This shares more with the Gnostics than with the Gospels. The Gnostics, an ancient school of thought, believed that creation mattered little, the body was bad, and the purpose of humans was to grasp "hidden knowledge" in order to escape the lower world—flesh, time, and matter.

The Bible foreshadows the final frame of the drama: Romans 8 talks about the liberation of creation from decay. 1 Corinthians 15 speaks of death being overcome. Revelation 21 and 22 talk about the renewed earth and the Heavenly

Jerusalem coming to earth. There is a hint that *this* world will be renewed. What if the idea was not the abolishment of space and time? What if the story leads to the kingdom coming to this earth?

The story of God's good creation leads us to believe that it wasn't version 1.0, something like a beta-version to be abolished when God thought of something better. This creation was his very good creation, and it has received his stamp of approval. The entire point we have forgotten is that God is faithful to his creation.

> *Jews were distinguished from their pagan neighbors ... There is nothing in the literature of Greece or Rome that remotely corresponds to what we find in Isaiah and the Psalms (Is 11:1–9; Ps 98:7–9).... A world set free from human injustice and from "natural" violence; a world in which oceans and mountains themselves rejoice at a new fulfilment; a world in which all people will celebrate the fact that very thing has been set right at last... This is not simply a hope beyond the world. It is a hope for the world.*[11]

The event in Jesus

How we misunderstood the Gospel

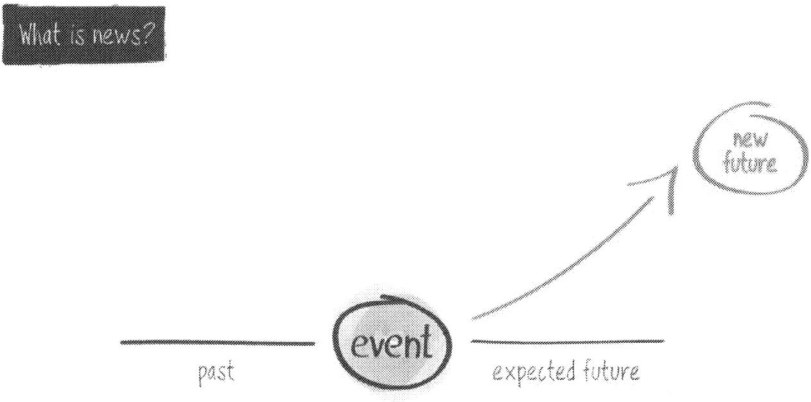

How news works: life cruises along, then something happens. That changes the direction of life.

WHEN we open a book of Tom's, we usually encounter steep claims. "We have not understood the Gospel," is as bold as one can claim. Isn't the Good News the basis and center of our faith? And we haven't understood it—how?

"In many churches," writes Tom in *Simply Good News*[12], "the good news has subtly changed into good advice: 'here's how to live, they say. Here's how to pray… Here's how to make sure you're on the right track for what happens after death … you won't go to hell; you'll go to heaven. Here's how to do it.' That is advice, not news."

News is about events that change the course of things. For example, a friend has a serious medical condition. After a visit to the doctor, he brims with joy since the latest findings declare him healthy. Something has happened (healing confirmed by the doctor's information) that changes the trajectory of life (not sickness, but health, and therefore new perspectives).

In ancient times, a gospel was a public announcement of change of rulership. The good news was that whatchamacallit had become emperor—hence life would be better. A gospel was a public statement about something that had happened.

If we look at churches up and down the road, we see this shortened Gospel. The preaching offers spiritual options to people. How life with God beats life without him. How we can avoid hell. How to live in this or that area.

The event of Jesus and his resurrection—that was news to the first believers. It changed the fate of Israel. Everything was different, all of a sudden. It changed the fate of the world. It changed the fate of individuals. Something was radically different. God was in charge. Caesar was not. That statement spread into all the world, a public faith that changed the Mediterranean countries like nothing before.

From personal to private religion

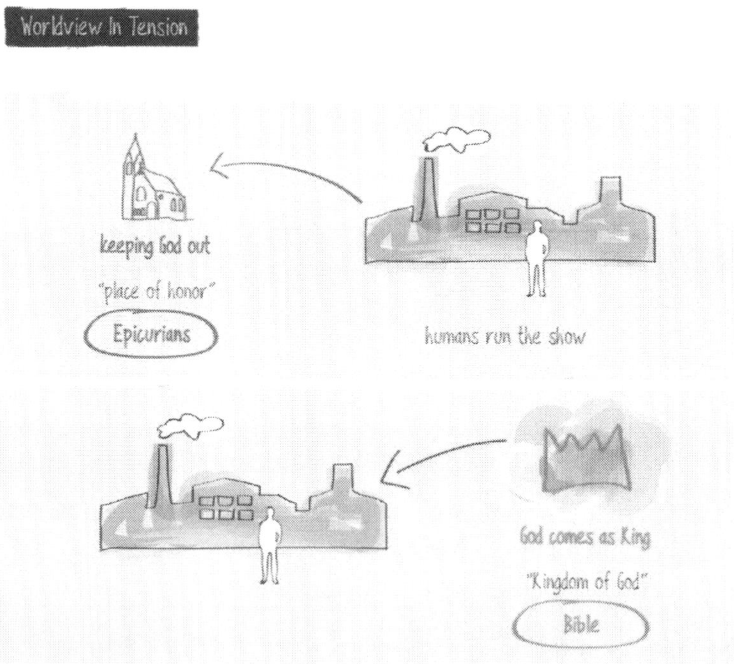

The tension in how we see the world. Our society loves to run the show and keep God out of the picture. It may give church a place of honor, but maintain clear separation of state and church. Jesus had a different idea: he came as king.

THESE days, I get sick if people tell me: "Faith is fine, as long as it helps you." As if Jesus were some sort of coping trick for a burdened life. The idea behind that sort of statement can be easy to track: there are many religions—who know which one is right? Why press religion on anybody. Let's just all be tolerant and let each person have his or her own way.

Well, fair. We should respect one another's preferences and not push our opinions onto others. I am all for that. This fits with the modern worldview of inner discovery and no absolutes. Maybe that is why Jesus as an option is easier to swallow than the event of Jesus.

The church has bought into this. From a religion of the heart, we have moved to a religion of "minding your own business." Personal religion has become private religion. God may have a place of honor in society, with churches and a few references here and there. Yet for all practical purposes, God is uninvited to our modern life, and humans are left to run the show.

We are not the first ones with this idea. The ancient Greeks came up with the idea of a "split" between heaven and earth. Epicur, a philosopher, lived about 350 years before Christ and got annoyed with all the God-stuff looming over life. His innovation: why don't we let the gods deal with heaven, while we humans rule the earth? Tom calls this "kicking God upstairs"—"God lives at the top of the building, and we live at the bottom; the stairs have been destroyed, and the elevators stopped working a long time ago."[13] In the eighteenth century, people plugged into the idea again with Enlightenment and the theory of evolution. God lives upstairs, and cares for "spiritual" things, while things down here are best left to natural laws, without any bothering with superstition or any kind of fanatic mingling.

The Bible claims that in Jesus, God became King. He has started to take charge. The event of Jesus means that we have a new boss in town. "A new state of affairs has been brought into existence. A door has been opened that nobody can shut. Jesus is now the world's rightful Lord, and all other lords are to fall at his feet."[14]

God arrived in history

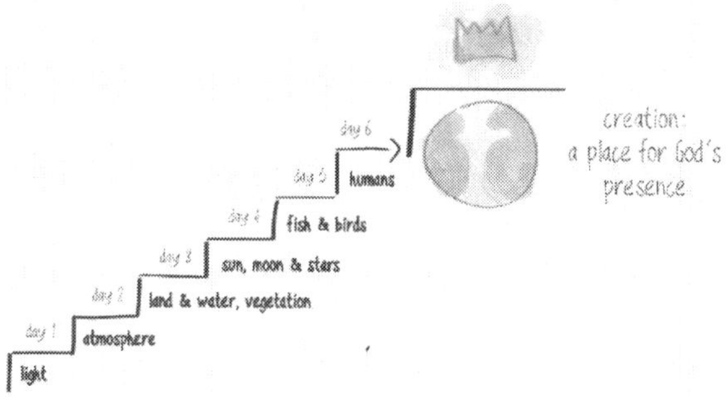

Immanuel—God is with us. It was there in creation, as God dwelt among people. It was there in the ark of the covenant. And it was the claim of Jesus: God came to dwell among his people.

LET'S look at another motive running through the Bible: God's presence. We see his presence in creation, then later in the Exodus, the Ark, and the Temple. Tom talks about the creation story with this motive:

The original creation story envisages a God who was making a dwelling place for himself. The six "days," or "stages" of creation indicate, to those who understand the world of the ancient Near East, that creation itself, heaven and earth together, is a kind of temple, a dwelling place for God.[15]

God living with his people. His presence with the people—this is the shalom the Bible talks about. The Bible ends in Revelation 22–23 on this note. "Immanuel" was bringing this perspective into human history.

In the very earliest Christian documents all pointed to a strange new reality: that, in Jesus, Israel's God had become present, had become human, had come to live in the midst of his people, to set up his kingdom, to take upon himself the full horror of their plight, and to bring about his long-awaited new world.[16]

This shows the turning point of history. From the moment of Jesus, everything was different. God dwelt with his people. The story changed. History ran in a different direction. The presence of God came as more than an inner fuzzy feeling or individual highlight. God is with his people—the day of the Lord has arrived. A new morning is here. The spirit is dwelling with communities. This really changes everything.

Easter speaks about this world

Which message did Easter send? Jesus is raised, therefore we have life after death, or: Jesus is raised, therefore he is Lord of the world.

EACH Easter millions of Christians celebrate the resurrection of Jesus. We celebrate the "new day." There is always a sense of completion with that moment. Tom makes an interesting observation about the reactions to the Easter event in the first century:

> *Despite a thousand Easter hymns and a million Easter sermons, the resurrection narratives in the gospels never, ever say anything like "Jesus is raised, therefore there is life after death," let alone, "Jesus is raised, therefore we shall go to heaven when we die."... No. Insofar as the event is interpreted, Easter has a very this-worldly, present-age meaning: Jesus is raised, so he is the Messiah, the world's true Lord; Jesus is raised, so God's new creation has begun—and we, his followers, have a job to do! Jesus is raised, so we must act*

as his heralds, announcing his lordship to the entire world, making his kingdom come on earth as in heaven![17]

The resurrection of Jesus was news, if there ever was news. It happened. And that statement and fact triggered all sorts of consequences. It meant not least that God was finally acting on his promises.

Let us recall the story structure of the Bible. We live in the fifth act of the Bible's story, the age of the church, and we are invited to play an active role in the story. As with any real play, we can improvise and shape the story. To live our part faithful and true to God's overall style and goal, we need to understand the early scenes well. "The biblical text is the primary authoritative source ("actors" should respect its plot-line, character development, and so on), but they must move beyond it if they are going to be faithful to it."[18] And then our actions drive the story toward the final scenes. We truly have a mission. God is on the move. And he has invited us to join.

What the kingdom of God means

The understanding before Tom

The main message of Jesus: The kingdom of God. That is what he talked about. That was his agenda.

JESUS spoke about the kingdom of God. This took the center stage in his proclamation and teaching. He arrived with it in Mark 1: "The time has come," he said. "The kingdom of God has come near. Repent and believe the good news!" And he took every opportunity to explain how it works.

How very strange that a lot of Christians cannot explain the kingdom of God in simple, straightforward sentences. Over the last forty years, this has picked up a bit. A theologian from Fuller Theological Seminary by the name of George Eldon Ladd played a central role in this. He published a book, *The Presence of the Future*, and explained that in Jesus the future has come forward into the present. The idea has found its way into popular expression with the phrase: *the now and the not yet*. We live in a time where the future is breaking in, but we also wait for a final consummation of all things. The technical term for this is *inaugurated eschatology* ("inauguration" being a ceremony that marks the beginning of a new term, and "eschatology" being the final events of history). The idea is that we participate in God's reign now already, and yet we wait for the final wrapping up of everything. Now-and-not yet.

Now-and-not-yet

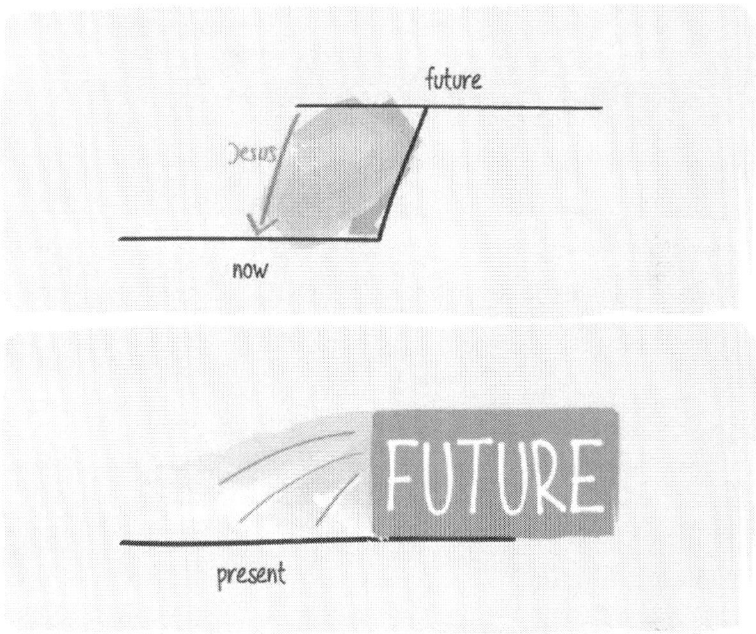

The now-and-not-yet understanding of the kingdom: God has made the age to come available in our times (the now). But not everywhere. It awaits consummation (the not-yet).

THE now-and-not-yet idea moved into the mainstream when John Wimber and the Vineyard picked it up. They built on Ladd's idea of what the kingdom means: (1) God's authority and right to rule and (2) the realm in which God exercises His authority. The kingdom meant a realm presently entered where we can experience God-stuff. For the Vineyard, this meant miracles, the presence of God, ministry to the poor, and a few other things.

This idea of spiritual perfection touching our earthly everyday drives Bethel, Vineyard, and many other charismatic groups. Most hold some of Ladd's ideas at the center. This was kingdom-understanding. Until Tom came along.

Tom fills the kingdom with a wider meaning. He goes deeper, more radical. He covers more ground in the Bible. And he gives us an understanding that is more shocking and disruptive than we have known so far.

The expectation: homecoming

One Creator God—that was the Jewish faith. The earth was good and made for him. This undercut all relativism claims of many gods or limited ability of God.

LET'S detour to the time before Christ once again. We need to start here to get the answer the Bible gives to the promises and hopes of Israel. The Jews held to the basic belief that God created everything and that he intended to fill his world with his love and care. The command to Adam and Eve was to "multiply and fill the earth." This command was repeated to Noah, Abraham, Jacob, Moses, the people of Israel, and Salomon. It seems God really wanted to fill the earth with his people.

God loves his creation. He cares for it. Seeing his handiwork causes the people to praise him. The Jews were soaked in a creation belief. Creation mattered because it showed God's brilliance and his care. And yet, things didn't always come together in harmony. Creation and the call of the covenant point to an inheritance in the world. The patriarchs were promised a place of goodness in a good creation.

And as we saw earlier, the covenant didn't pan out as they thought. The unfaithfulness of Israel meant that the chosen people ended up in exile. Yet that was surely just a phase. The story had a different ending. "The day of the Lord" remained the hope for Israel. One day, God would act and put an end to exile.

The story of Israel...

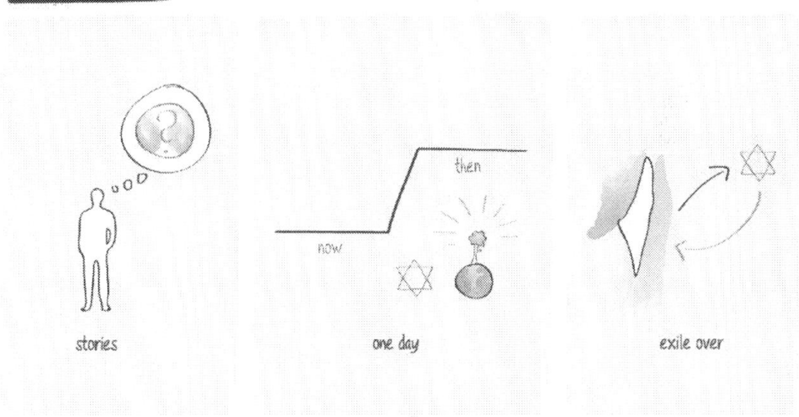

The story of Israel: they were called but waited on something. They believed in the one day when God would come and bring the blessing he had promised. One day, exile would be over. One day, the promises would be fulfilled.

The prophets pointed to the earth being blessed and the nation in it: scattered people brought home, fig trees, security, streams of water, and the glory of God everywhere. Creation lay as the basis for the Jewish faith. Creation expressed God's care. God had promised to fill it. God intended to restore the fortunes of his people. God brought peace and homecoming to people. Let's see how that picks up in the New Testament.

The answer: new creation

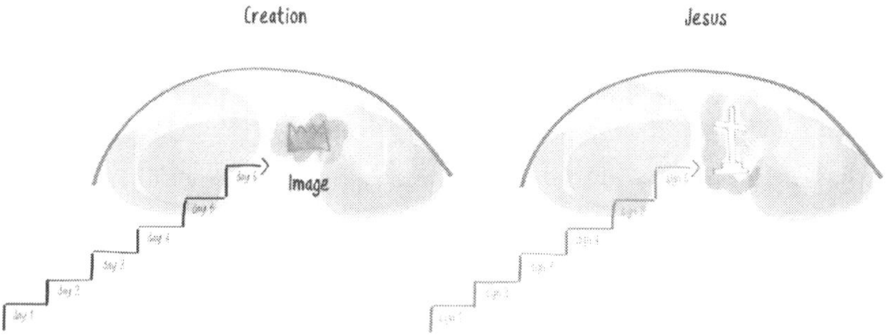

In creation, after six days, God placed man as his own image in the garden. The Gospel of John shares six signs, and then the "son of man" is placed on the cross as the "King of the Jews." John picks creation as his story and leads us to see new creation arriving in the work on the cross.

JOHN'S Gospel stands as a towering text in the history of mankind. He kicks his Gospel off with Jesus as the creator: "in the beginning was the word…"[19] Jesus is logos—the logos created. John sets the scene for Jesus by anchoring his story in the creation story.

Next, Jesus comes into his creation. Incarnation: "the word became flesh and dwelled amongst us."[20] God comes into his handiwork to redeem it. Change comes from within.

Jesus goes to his death in order to complete the work of dealing with the evil ***within*** *the existing creation and thereby opening the possibility for the new creation to be born*[21]

The cross comes as the crucial game-changer in the history of creation. John devotes many chapters to the cross and the events surrounding it. Here, we see ongoing echoes from creation:

Genesis 1, read by an ancient near-easterner, would be understood as a description of the building of a temple. God, in the six days of creation, is building himself a place to dwell. The final work he does in creation is to create an image of himself, an *eikon,* and place it in the temple. This image would assist the worshippers by reminding them of who it is they are there for. This *eikon,* in Genesis, is Adam. This happens *on the sixth day.*

John takes us on a tour of signs: the wedding at Cana, "the first sign" (2:11); healing the centurion's servant, "this was the second sign" (4:46–54); the pool at Bethesda (chapter 5); the feeding of the five thousand (chapter 6); the healing of the man born blind (chapter 9); and raising Lazarus (chapter 11). "Six signs in the first half of the Gospel, from chapter 1–12. After that we move to the upper room.... What, no more signs? What is the seventh sign?"[22]

Fast forward to John 19. Jesus' final day. The preparation for the Passover, the celebration of delivery from oppression. Friday. *The sixth day of the week.* Jesus stands accused. He has been brought before Pilate. The torture has already begun, the crown of thorns pressed onto his head, the purple robe draped over him in mockery. Finding no guilt in him, Pilate brings him before the crowds and declares, "Behold the Man!"

The "temple" being built now is the architecture of salvation, the new creation, a community of saints with Jesus as the *eikon*, the final placement, the image of God. The true Man does what Adam was not able to do, what Israel was not able to do. The true Royal Priest is here. "We beheld his glory," says John.[23]

Jesus as the true man, completing creation. This thought is picked up later by Paul, who labels Jesus as the "new Adam." Creation completed and remade.

On the cross, Jesus ends with "it is finished"—echoing the steps of creation in Genesis 1. On the day of resurrection, the women mistake Jesus for the gardener—"the right mistake to make because like Adam he is charged with bringing God's new world to order."[24] Jesus as working in God's garden. Creation echoes again.

> *The claim advanced in Christianity is of that magnitude: that with Jesus of Nazareth there is not simply a new religious possibility, not simply a new ethic or a new way of salvation, but a new creation.*[25]

John gives us a clear commitment to creation in presenting Christ. Creation is completed and changed.

The new in the middle of the old

The Jewish Hope

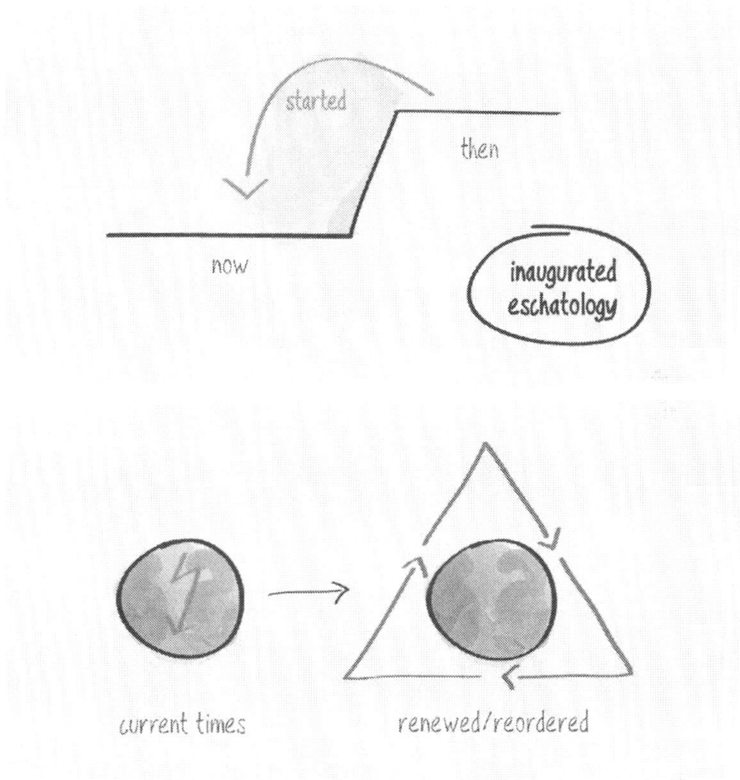

The Jewish hope was that one day the world would be put right. Jesus' claim was that in him that started. The future arrived in the present. The King has come. New creation has started.

THE early Christians really believed that the world had turned upside down. In Jesus of Nazareth, the new creation launched. This was more than a better religious life free of pressure. This was more than an empowered moral code. This was more than personal salvation. This was new creation!

And yet the timing was curious. Jews did believe that the dead would rise—at the end of time. No one imagined a resurrection in the middle of history. Jews believed that there would be a large-scale event that happened to everyone and to all God's people. But one person being raised ahead of the rest was stunning!

What does that mean? The end has come. The day of the Lord is here. "The main point of the resurrection is that it is the beginning of God's new world."[26] The new world is launched. But in the middle of the old. That seems crazy. How could God split up the cleaning-the-world operation? Well, he did. And he stuck to his original idea: creation and humans playing a role as stewards of his purposes.

> *God's future has come forward to meet us in the present; what God intends to do at the last has already broken into the world the way it is.... We are with the early Christians, celebrating the fact that part one of that great event has already happened in the resurrection of Jesus and the outpouring of the Spirit, and looking forward eagerly to part two, when what began at Easter and Pentecost will at last be completed.*[27]

Now, the resurrection speaks to two things: God's commitment to renewing creation, as well as his claim over all creation. He inaugurated his reign on earth. We are seeing the end in the present. Jesus' body was raised. He is the firstborn, for many to follow. In Jesus, the future has come into our time.

This is the kingdom: new creation—the reign of God over his creation. This is more than a spiritual invasion from another dimension. The kingdom is material. It happens in time and space. God became King, and we are part of it!

This is the kingdom

Jesus' message of the kingdom of God connects to the long story leading up to his birth. That story pointed to a promise and to a new future. The hope is now fulfilled: God is in charge.

LET us come now to a refreshed understanding of the kingdom. Tom thinks: "I firmly believe that part of this task in our generation is to alert the church to the theme of the kingdom."[28] When Jesus kicked off his public career he claimed, "the time is fulfilled. The Kingdom of God is here."[29] He went around and preached "the Gospel of the kingdom" (as in Mk 1:13; Mt 4:23; Lk 4:43). What exactly is the kingdom of God?

The classical understanding over the last generation ran like this: The kingdom of God is the reign and rule of God. The dynamic action of the King over his subjects.

Tom takes this a step further. He highlights that the kingdom is the God-in-charge project, not just of willing people but as an announcement for all creation.

The kingdom of God means today what it always meant. According to Jesus, God is now in charge of the world in a whole new way. God is redemptively in charge.[30]

The kingdom means more than a realm within which to experience God for the willing. It means a change in affairs. A new management being installed in the world. A change in times and in the course of history. For everyone, willing or unwilling.

The kingdom operates differently than anything we had expected: no enforcement, no new power play. The way of self-giving love shows the nature of the King and his kingdom. Jesus said, it is here. We are living in this new time.

A new take on morals

Chasing happiness

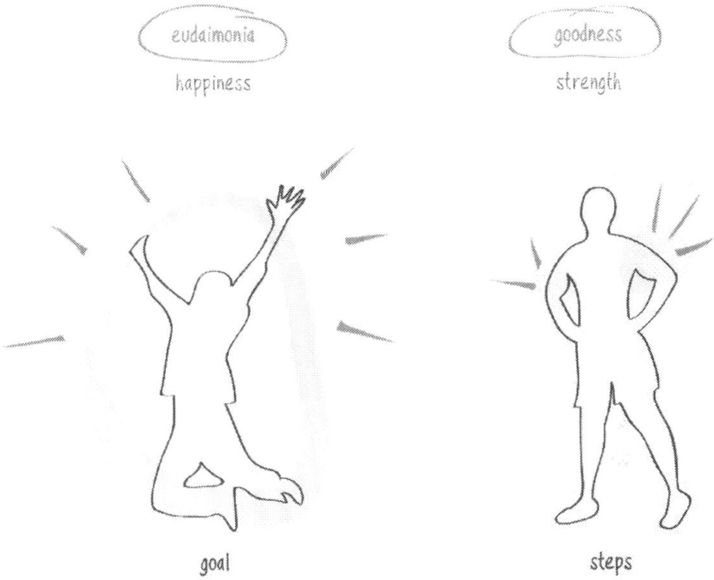

For the ancient philosophers like Aristotle, the goal of life was human flourishing and happiness. You get there through two things: a clear goal, and certain steps toward it. The goal is happiness. The steps are character strengths—virtues—used to reach that goal.

"IF it makes you happy, it can't be that bad," sings Sheryl Crow. She captures the attitude of many modern people. Feelings and the freedom to pursue whatever you find helpful and delightful matter. Freedom reigns—and the church has bought into it. The demand of individual fulfillment seems to be at the core of what people understand as moral. Life is good when it feels good.

Even though some Christian literature says that "it's not about you," most sermons, most advice, most motivation do feed this notion. Christian hedonism buys into this and gives it a coat of God-color. Christian romanticism sets inner feelings above any real reflection or call for discipline.

The Greeks came up with the original idea. It was Aristotle who proposed *Eudaimonia*—the pursuit of happiness as the original form of the good life. His teaching showed how the virtues (good behavior) support this ultimate goal of human flourishing. That sounds like a lot of today's pop-psychology and pop-sermons.

The reaction in church can be stern and uptight. Forget happiness—behave properly. And the school of discipline tries to convey clear morals because God demands it (while still emphasizing grace). A tough job.

We are looking at the wrong place, says Tom. Self-fulfillment is not the ultimate goal; reflecting the image of God stands as our purpose as humans. Being restored into the way he intended and living in accordance with God's new creation should be our ultimate goal.

> *Aristotle glimpsed a goal of human flourishing; so did Jesus, Paul, and the rest. But Jesus's vision of that goal was larger and richer, taking in the whole world, and putting humans not as lonely individuals developing their own moral status but as glad citizens of God's coming kingdom.*[31]

In the story of the Bible, humans find happiness in the happiness of everything else. Human happiness is no isolated ship that sails into utter freedom. The good life of the Christian is found in the Shalom of God—a good ordering and running of everything God created. As such, Christians not only builds their own place in the world, but look beyond themselves.

> *The glory of virtue, in the Christian sense, is that the self is not in the center of that picture. God and God's kingdom are in the center. As Jesus himself said, we are to seek first God's kingdom and his justice*[32]

It's not about you. Really.

Forget happiness, you are called to a throne

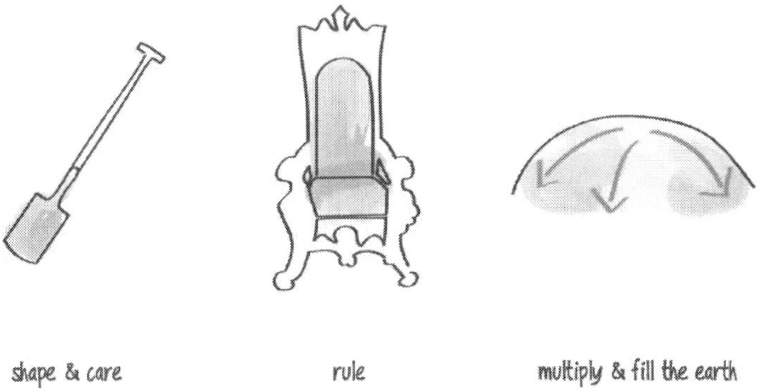

The idea of God's image has three aspects: to till the garden, to rule, and to multiply into all the earth.

THE story of the Bible leads us to the kingdom of God. We are stunned by the new creation bursting on the scene in Jesus. Let's look at the original picture of us humans in creation. There, we were designed in God's image. We were put in charge of God's created order. And being fully human meant living in this design. For Aristotle, humans reached for *eudaimonia*; for the creator they reached for the *image of God*.

Forget happiness, you are called to a throne. God intends to run the world with and through us. This is picked up in the New Testament. Again, we have the idea of working with God in his world. Of spreading the kingdom. Of being stewards under his rule. Collaborative eschatology—working with God to draw heaven to earth.

And how does that play out? By virtue. By the development of Christian character. By imitation of Jesus. By the fruit of the Spirit. These concepts all speak about the same role: maturing as a person to play a role in God's new world.

The world created in Genesis is designed as a world that reproduces. Plants, animals, humans—everything and everyone recreates itself. We are sharing in the creative work of God. God works through humans. As God created the world, he put humans in place as stewards of his creation. We are images of God. As such, we have a threefold purpose: to shape and maintain the world, to rule over it, and to multiply and spread.

"New creatures" is what Paul calls us (Galatians 6:15; 2 Corinthians 5:17). This means that the original purpose has been put back into place. We live the three-fold purpose again.

Creation is an open project

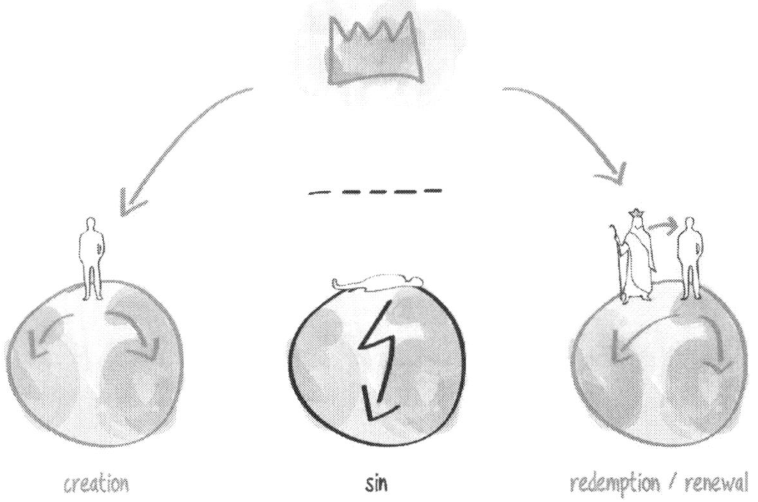

The Christian story of morals is about ruling in God's world. People need good character to be good stewards and act out God's goodness.

WE are called to play a part in God's new creation as faithful servants, part of a royal priesthood, stewarding God's creation and reflecting worship back to him. Our growth as Christians enables us to share God's stewardship. We open the door to be good news for the world. We reflect God's image once again into his world. We share the reign of God.

This is an open project, as Tom says. No predetermined pathways. More a collaboration between the creator and his creatures.

Creation waits for humans to pick up their responsibility. Romans 8 talks about the effects of sin on creation itself. Creation suffers. Once humans start to act out their God-design, creation will celebrate. We undo the sin of Adam that got the whole world off track.

To be saved means much more than to have a personal relationship with God. Saved people save the world. Tom highlights this connection very keenly: "The crucial factor in Jesus's kingdom project picks up the crucial factor in God's creation project. God intended to rule the world through human beings."[33] Jesus picks up the calling of Adam. As we figure out what Jesus has done, it will impact the world around us. It will play into the design that God has for his creation. God redeems people to redeem the world.

Preparing to participate in God's project

Ethics Follows the Image of God

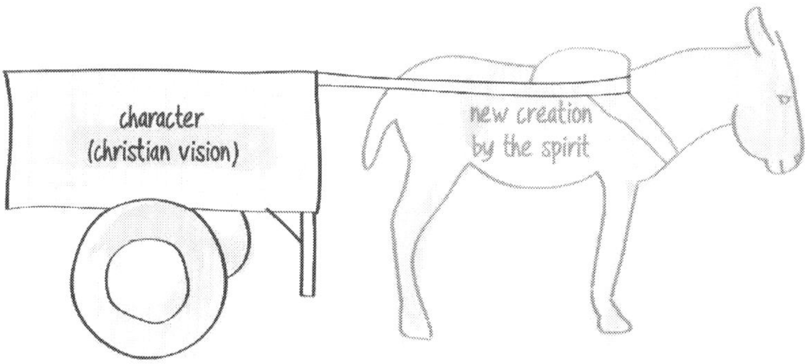

Don't put the cart before the horse. The understanding of Christian character grows out of the vision of God's new world created by the Spirit.

SWITCHING off the TV, it can sometimes be hard to believe the claim that humans are formed in the image of God. There is so much greed, so much war, and so much disrespect in our world. Is every person really a reflection of the good Creator?

Humans don't always represent God's image. Even though everyone is made in his image, our individual choices and lifestyles can hide that fact. Sin corrupts God's image in us. Through the work of Jesus, sin is judged and its effects overcome. After a cleansing, the purpose can be picked up again.

It is time to focus on morals—how character works. The attitudes and behaviors of humans either reflect God's character or they hide his image. The key to understanding the role of character lies in looking at new creation. This is the ultimate vision of the early Christians: humans act as stewards and co-creators in God's new world. Through this, we understand morals and the way our character can be formed.

Character follows the image-of-God idea. Once we understand character in the light of new creation and our role in it as co-reigning with God, morals become very important. Tom warns us to get that order right: new creation, then character. The other way around would put the cart before the horse. Only with the right order do we get a way of discussing character and morals that doesn't drift to taste and individual experiences.

The way we live is not just about avoiding punishment, following a set of arbitrary rules, or pulling ourselves together. The way we live enables us to spread God's glory. Or not.

Reflecting God into the world

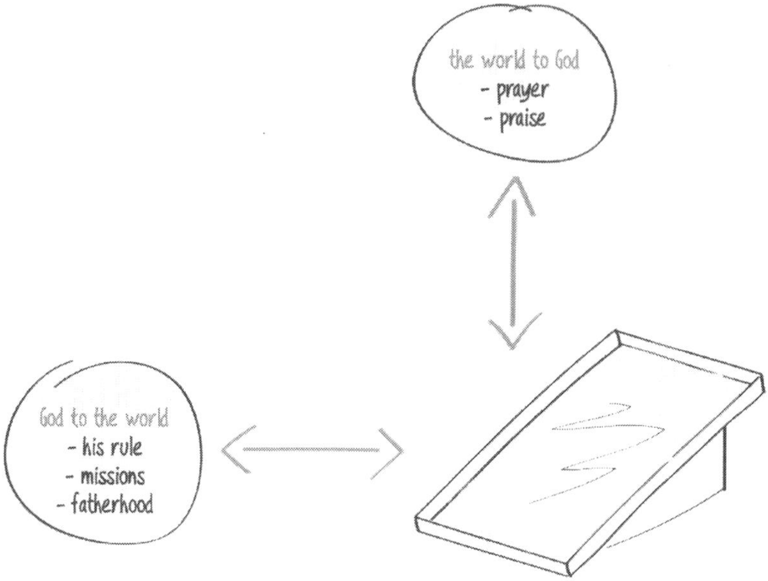

Being in God's image is like being an angled mirror. We reflect God's rule into the world and gather the good deeds in praise to God.

"We are like an angled mirror," says Tom. As images of God, we reflect God into the world. We can call this "missions." We bring the glory of God to the world. This is what it means to "rule," in a Christian sense: to be a wise steward to God's creation.

The mirror goes the other way as well. We reflect the world back to God. In prayer and praise, we shine God's goodness back to him, and ask for his guidance on the problems of our world.

> *The image is a vocation, a calling. It is the call to be an angled mirror, reflecting God's wise order into the world and the praises of all creation back to the creator. That is what it means to be the royal priesthood: looking after God's world is the royal bit; summing up creation's praise is the priestly bit.* [34]

> *All this is contained in the idea of being remade in God's image. The point of a mirror isn't that it's useful or beautiful in itself, but that it reflects the face of one who looks into it. The point of an angled mirror is that it reflects one thing to another: in this case, God to the world (mission) and the world back to God (worship).*[35]

Holiness links worship and mission. The angled mirror has to be clean in order to perform. Holiness keeps the image uncontaminated, so that the link between God and the world actually works. That is our destiny.

Moral guidance comes through getting the story right: God's good creation filled with humans as his wise stewards and Jesus launching new creation and putting humans as his kingdom agents in charge of his new-creation project. Our moral conversations flow from the ideas of God's creation and the nature of his kingdom. They will find their full flavor in the lives lived as part of that story. As a community of prayer and engagement in shaping God's world, we will find our voice again and speak to the hope of God's beautiful design.

Part Three. The Story Changed

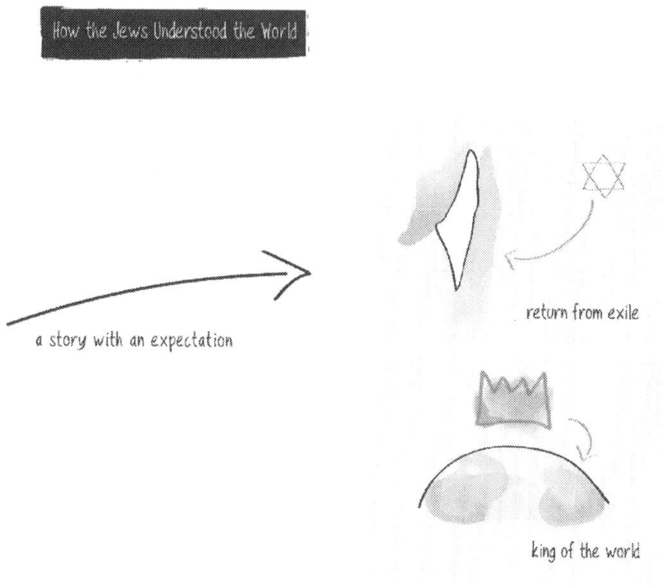

This is the story of the Jews that Jesus answered. They waited for a return from exile. In Jesus, that happened and God became King of the world.

WE have looked at Tom's fresh insights and why he rocks the world of theology. We've also seen four insights that come with a unique spin from his studies:

1) The Bible connects a story with God at the center and Torah as the beginning of the solution
2) The Jesus event changed the world and cannot be reduced to a private option
3) The kingdom of God states that God's new creation has begun in our time
4) We are partners in God's renewal of all things as his image-bearers

These gifts from Tom refresh our view on the Bible. No longer do we tell a story about solving the problems of individuals, whether those problems are distance from an angry God or an inability to find harmony and a good life. No, we hear a story about God. A story about fulfilment. A story about homecoming and return from exile. A story about a new kind of King. God is the actor. He has his plans. And they include us.

What does this story mean for us? To this we shall turn now...

A new pair of eyes to see – a New Testament worldview

How the mind is transformed

In the transformation of the mind, we dive into God's story and find new answers to who and where we are.

I WAS reading the paper the other day and it included a piece on how the price for secondary education has skyrocketed. MBAs and other college degrees have become super expensive, and this cost is only increasing. Knowledge and disciplined ways of thinking make a big difference in our world. It turns out that the early Christians put a similarly high value on the way we think.

The logic goes like this: Renewing the world starts with renewed people. The renewal of people hinges on a renewed mind. A new mindset is therefore the decisive factor in living with Christ. Let's look at some of his writings and how the mind is emphasized there:

Romans starts by saying, *"their thinking became futile"* (1:21), then tells the great story of Christ, Israel, and redemption, tying it all together with, *"therefore, be transformed by the renewing of your mind"* (12:2).

Ephesians prays that, *"the eyes of your understanding be enlightened"* (1:18), calls unbelievers, *"darkened in their understanding"* (4:18), and calls us to *"be made new in the attitudes of your mind"* (4:23).

Philippians says, *"Let the mind of Christ be in you"* (2:5). Colossians urges us, *"to set the mind on things above"* (3:2). First Corinthians confirms, *"we have the mind of Christ"* (2:16).

The list could go on and on. The way we think matters. A Christian mindset contrasts with one that doesn't know God. And the Bible is more than a set of rules or creeds that set the boundaries of our faith. The Bible is a story that invites us to join the story. The Gospels and the letters of the New Testament invite us to think theologically ourselves. We are called into a process that transforms our very assumptions and what we have been taught previously.

Train the mind, says Tom. We engage in the story of God, find our place in it, and put our minds to figuring out what that means for us. This requires concentration, practice, discussion, prayer, immersion in Scripture, and engagement in thought.

Don't suppose for a minute that grace will work without your mind being fully engaged. Here we find it yet again: God wants us to be people, not puppets; real human beings who think things out and make actual decisions, not straws in the wind to be blown this way and that. You need to "figure out properly things that differ."[36]

The Spirit will guide us. He reveals the thoughts of God to us and he builds on our willingness to put in the effort. To this we now turn as we look at worldviews …

How worldviews work

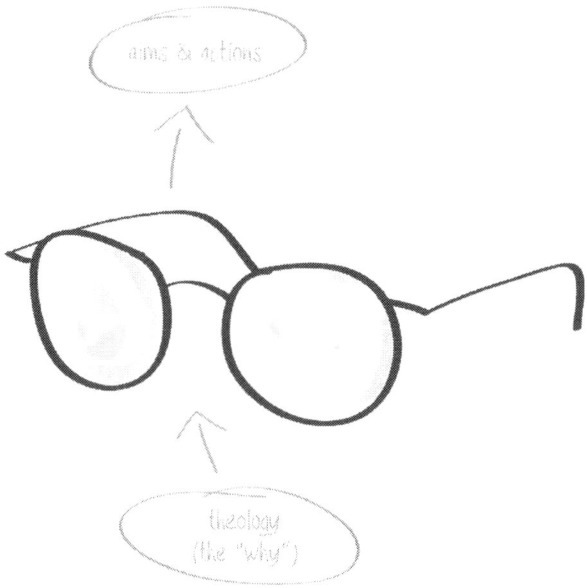

Worldviews are like a set of glasses—you look through them to understand the world. They are built of the stories we tell ourselves, of key symbols we take for granted, of a set of practices and they answer five questions.

"A WORLDVIEW is the thing you look through," says Tom, "not at."[37] He makes the comparison to a set of glasses. They help you see. They focus things. And usually, they are not noticed when used. Other people might see them, but the wearer has trouble being aware of them or analyzing them.

In every culture, there seems to be a common set of assumptions that can't be questioned. That is the worldview in operation. "Well, in this day and age, we see things ..." is a typical worldview phrasing. Nothing much needs to be explained. It is just the way things are—for that culture.

Maybe we are often fooled by our own assuredness. It is time to take a look at our glasses. That is Tom's advice.

So how do they work? There are three elements and a set of questions:

- *Stories*, a set of symbols and practices, make up the worldview. The narrative explains how we came to this point in history and where we are headed.

- *Symbols* are things that we couldn't think of doing without, like a flag (imagine someone burning a US flag—a key symbol that stands for a way of life).
- The *praxis* reinforces the story and symbols—it's what people collectively do and value in a culture; what "good taste" they assume and what is taken for granted.

Additionally, there is a set of five questions that give shape to a worldview:

- Who are we?
- Where are we?
- What is wrong?
- What is the solution?
- What time is it?

Sound complicated? Well, a few examples might help ...

Worldview of the twenty-first century

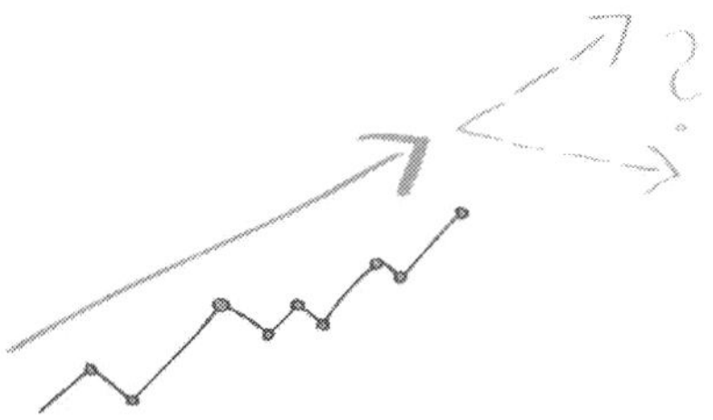

Progress
running out of steam

Captain of my own boat

The story of the Western mindset: we are advanced and progress further. We captain our own boats into freedom and self-expression.

LET'S take our own day and age as an example. While our world covers a wide range of ideas and cultures, there might be a common view in the West. Tom proposes the following:

Story: We basically tell a story of progress. Out of the eighteenth-century Enlightenment we put science and technology at the center and promised a forward-march in history. Things got better. Yet, this progress ran into trouble because of our inability to solve big problems: we killed millions in the last century in the West, we fired atom bombs, our systems suffer under human greed and misconduct, and 9/11 showed that other forces will not be leaving us in peaceful progress land anytime soon. So, our progress remains, but we have run out of steam and are searching for new direction. ,We also tell a story of choices and freedom. The current mood can be expressed in the phrase "captain my own soul." We seek self-fulfillment and an organization to our lives that puts our personal tastes foremost.

> *Our culture has gotten fixated on self-realization. On discovering who I truly am, and then being true to that. That is one of the major cultural imperatives that we have. And a lot of people think that is basically what Jesus taught. Jesus really told exactly the opposite: if you want to find yourself, you have to lose yourself.*[38]

Symbols: Money is a symbol, for sure. The more we have, both in value and in power and status, the more we are esteemed. Our cities are dominated by a skyline that speaks of great business and money structures. We have bought in to compound interest, where the multiplication of money is its own reward, with no real target behind it other than wealth accumulation.

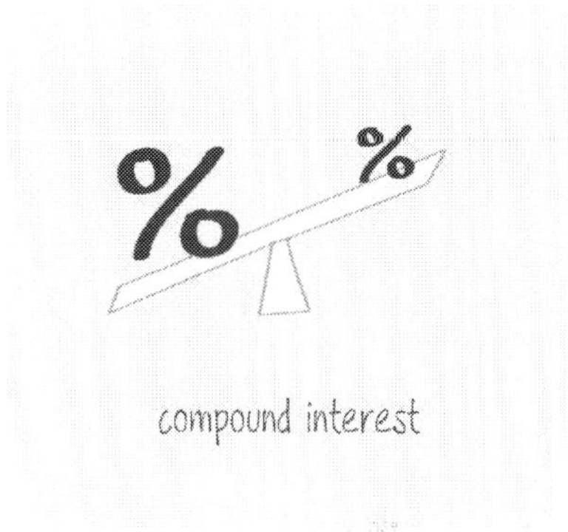

The symbols of the Western mindset: money as a means of influence and self-fulfillment. Compound interest as a story of progress.

Praxis: *Tesco, ergo sum* (I shop, therefore I am). That seems to be a new mantra for our day. It gives people a sense of power, of being able to do things, and of captaining their own boat. We travel at an unprecedented rate, and seek experiences in multiple ways. As we go, we take our values with us, both in the franchises we set up the world over and in our personal tastes and understanding of how power should work. Democracy for all—that is our ambition and hope for the world.

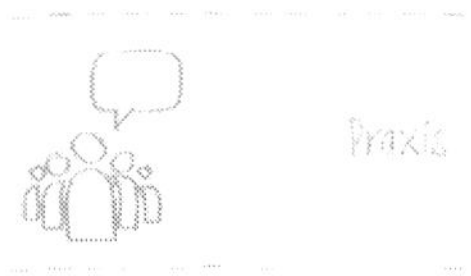

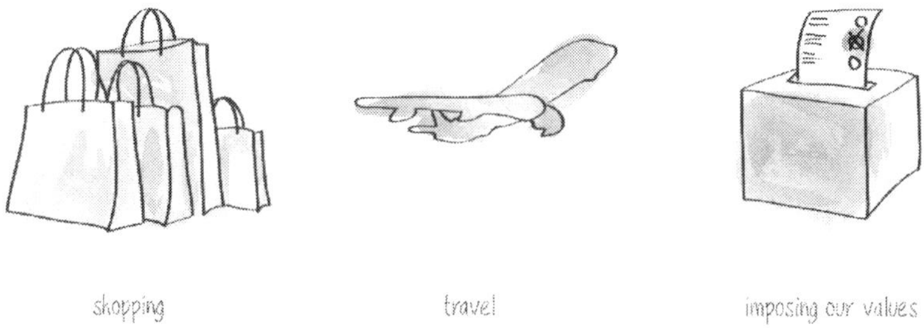

The praxis of the Western mindset: shopping, travel, and imposing our values, such as democracy and equality, on the world.

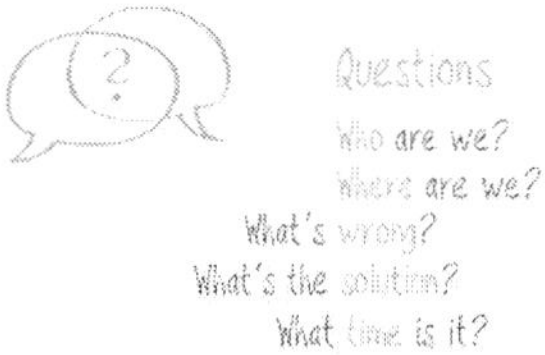

The questions:

Who are we: We are intelligent people. People with resources and a good education. We have made it.

Where are we: We are in an uncertain world. As much as we would like to have stability and peace, there seem to be issues we can't fully solve.

What is wrong: Tyrannies. Ideologies with a totalitarian claim. We don't like religion that claims absolute authority, and we don't like dictators who can't be predicted and integrated into our value systems.

What is the solution: The solution is a mix between hope, war, media, and soft pressure. Imposing our values on the world still is favorite idea. Education, media, and business can carry our values to all cultures.

What time is it: We are in uncertain times, unfortunately. We would like there to be more safety and freedom, but we are not there yet.

OK, this summarizes our day and age. How about the times of Jesus? How did the apostle Paul view the world?

Worldview of Paul

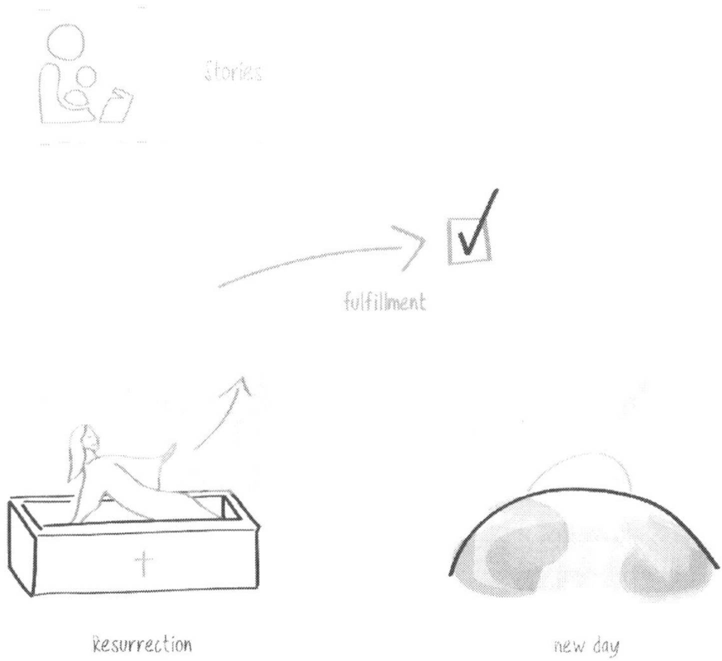

The story of Paul smacks of fulfillment. A long journey finally reached its destiny. The resurrection is the key turning point—it means that the new day has dawned. God has finally acted and brought the conclusion to all yearnings and hopes.

TOM spends much of his work developing insights into the mindset of the apostle Paul. As Tom says, "Having the mind of the Messiah means being in tune with the idea of new creation. For the ancient philosophers, thinking was about being in tune with the way the world really was. For Paul, it was about being in tune with the way the world was supposed to be with God's new creation."[39] This drift toward new creation is anchored in the worldview of Paul. Upon which *story* did Paul's view on the world build? There are three aspects to that story.

Fulfillment: Paul picked up the story of the Old Testament and said that it was coming to completion in Jesus. He drew on the hopes of the Jews that God would one day come to his people, that he would end exile, and that he would be with his people. The New Testament claims that it *happened.*

Inaugurated eschatology: The Jews were looking for this great day of the Lord's return as "the Lord's day," and they expected it to happen at the end of time. Then everything would be over. Paul told that story. But with a twist. It happened. But everything wasn't over. The end has come forward into our time. The kingdom broke into this age. New creation crashed into history. We live in the overlap of the ages—the now and not yet.

God becoming King: God came as judge and redeemer into the now. A new day had dawned. People would be forgiven. Sin would be judged. The kingdom was here. And God started to rule. Not yet completely. Not yet everywhere. But for real. In the here. In the now. For those who believed the message. For those who submitted to his will.

With that story, what were the *symbols* in Paul's view?

The unity and holiness of the church. A community that centers around Jesus as King. A community that is reconciled with and loves one another. Here lie the keys to Paul's worldview. The community replaced the temple as the place where heaven and earth met—this was now happening in gatherings and relationships of disciples.

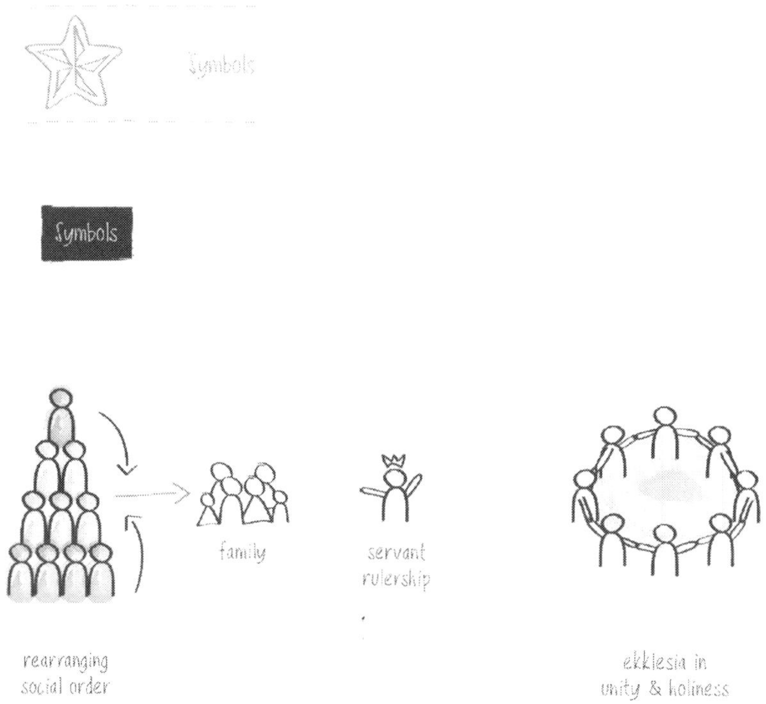

The symbols of Paul's worldview: A new social order where people act as family. Even leadership is redefined into servanthood. The cross as the key turning point in history. The unity and holiness of the church under one God.

> *Paul isn't interested in having some Messiah followers from this group, and some meeting over there from that particular social bracket. Paul wants them all to worship together. That is the sign in front of the watching world that Jesus really is the Lord of the world, and is not simply the lord of some cult here that you can follow this way if you like, or that way if you like. You are to be united across all the traditional social and cultural boundaries*[40]

With that comes a reordering of the social structure. While the world around him took great pains to maintain stability by keeping everyone in their place, Paul reordered social standing into one big family. The powerful were called to servanthood. The slaves were turned into brothers and sisters. The lowly found their place alongside the rich. All were on level ground, just as promised in Isaiah.

Which *praxis* goes with that?

In this new age, we live as renewed humans. This offers healing and renewal, and calls for both holiness and dedication to God's world-saving plans. For Paul, this changed the way we think, act and feel. Reconciliation plays a key role in this: it sustains communities. It also calls the larger world with the message that in Christ "all things" will be reconciled to him.

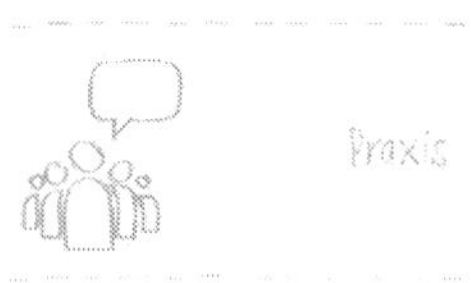

Praxis

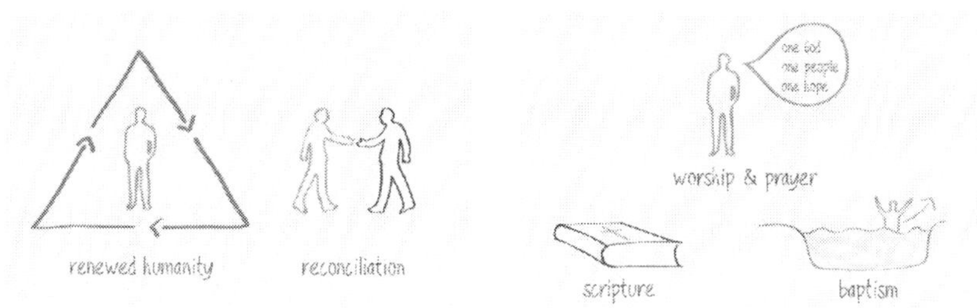

The praxis of Paul's worldview: Renewed individuals and reconciliation in all relationships. Worship and prayer that announced one God, one people, and one hope. Scripture and baptism confirm the underlying story.

Worship and prayer as key activity of the church are found at the center of Paul's worldview. These are to be done with a glad heart, especially if we think about all that happened and where we now live. The practice of reading und thinking through Scripture enables the transformation of our minds in such a way as to allow us to figure out this day of new arrival. And baptism was the sign of the new covenant, of resurrection happening for those who follow Jesus.

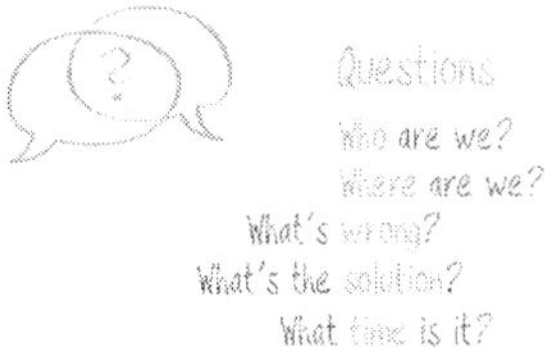

What about the *five questions*:

Who are we: We are one people. We are the in-Messiah people. We are the people of the new covenant, included in God's saving acts.

Where are we: We are in the world, part of God's new creation. Jesus reigns in the world. God is King in our world.

What is wrong: Sin, Caesar, old humanity. People are corrupted and the world is still bent out of shape. People are in rebellion and fail to see the Messiah.

What is the solution: Prayer, the work of the spirit, resurrection, preaching Jesus as King. All of these will aid the spread of the renewing work of God and his kingdom.

What time is it: New Creation Time. We witness the overlap of the ages. God's time has dawned on us. It is time to put his new creation into effect.

Look at this and compare it to the mindset around you. What stories, symbols, praxis, and questions do we hear around us? Even Christians seem miles away from this view of things. It might be time to take off our old glasses and refocus on what is really going on.

Why we all think God lives upstairs

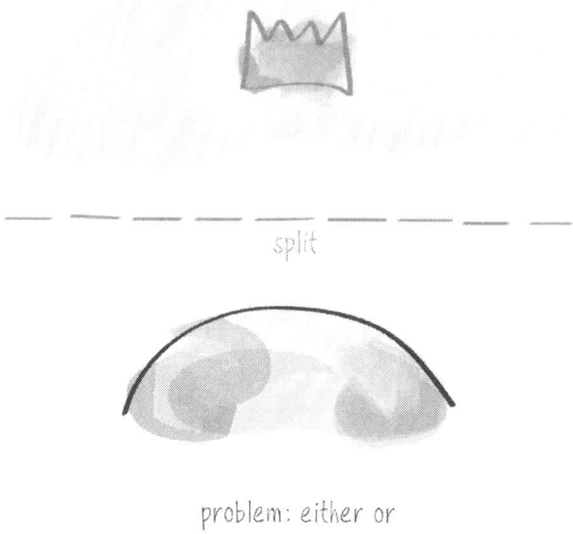

The big problem of the Western mindset: assuming that God lives far apart from us. That leads to all sorts of dualities.

How come we are stuck with a copy of the world's mind? Tom points to the ancient Greek philosophy we saw earlier: Epicureanism. The idea gives us glasses that are so powerful that we interpret everything through them, even the Bible.

The reference to Epicurus runs through all of Tom's writing ("God lives at the top of the building, and we live at the bottom; the stairs have been destroyed, and the elevators stopped working a long time ago"[41]). The split level of a world that runs separate from God creates all sorts of difficulty. It powers the modern self-understanding. And it blocks the light that would allow us to see the Gospel for what it is.

> *What prevents us from thinking in these terms is the long and often unrecognized triumph of a modern version of the ancient philosophy called*

Epicureanism. As long as we are thinking in that way, with God or the gods a long way away and earth trundling on entirely by its own steam, we will never glimpse that vision. As long as we are still in awe of the great Scottish philosopher David Hume, who declared that miracles don't happen because they can't happen, we will not only find it difficult to believe in the ancient Jewish worldview. We will find it difficult even to understand what it was about.[42]

The split-level blinds us to the overall story of God running the world. Even a belief in miracles might be based on a split-level understanding, the surprise being that God shows up, which he really rarely does. A similar hidden split-level can drive the question: was something from God or from man? Was it effort or was it God working? This is a question a split-level worldview asks. Someone who sees God as being intimately involved with all creation would not need to choose.

Our culture has a story about progress, about possessions, about position in a safe world. That seems self-evident and hard to question. However, it runs counter to the Bible. The story of God has a different hope. A story about God's new world. A hope in resurrection. A task to spread God's glory by reflecting his image into all streets. Which story are you buying? Which story are you living?

What we can't see

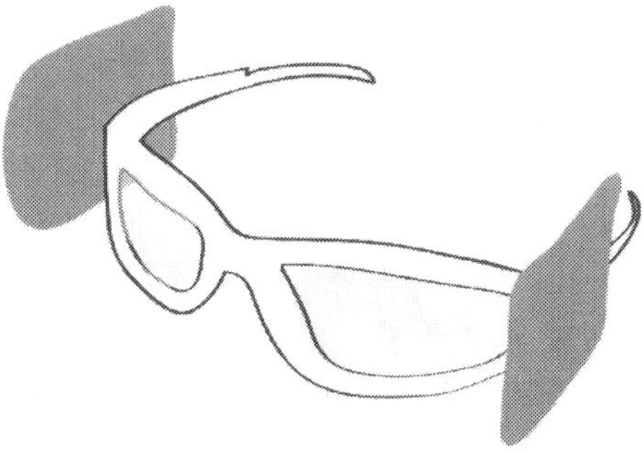

The shades on our Western worldview—the Epicurean assumption that we all hold.

WORLDVIEWS sound a bit complicated. Whoever thinks like that? True, this does not feature a lot in discussions in homes, the media, or the churches. Once you look at the great conflict of our time, however, the question of worldview seems very relevant. Even if they don't come up in discussion, the world's battles are worldview battles. Take the example of militant Islam versus materialism, or look at the continuing conflicts between China, Russia, Israel, and the United States. Each nation holds different visions of how things should work. Their stories, symbols, praxis, and questions lead them to very different conclusions. Whenever they cross paths, we see another tension building in our world.

Jesus came with a story and an announcement that was difficult to fit in for the people of his time. Their worldview had no space for a God coming into human history, for a God dying on a cross, and for resurrection to happen while the rest of the world drags on.

> *The God who has raised Jesus from the dead within history, leaves evidence that demands an explanation from the scientist as well as anybody else. Insofar as I understand scientific method, when something turns up that doesn't fit the paradigm you're working with, one option at least, perhaps when all others have failed, is to change the paradigm, not to exclude everything you've known to that point but to include it within a larger whole.*[43]

We in our times have similar problems fitting the Jesus story into our story. "To believe in the resurrection of Jesus is simply impossible for those who accept current paradigms of reality... What is at stake is the clash between a worldview that allows for a God of creation and justice, and worldviews that don't."[44]

Tom criticizes modern reading of the Bible as submitting to a cultural worldview of the West—the story of a God uninvolved in daily affairs. If God is detached from daily life, even the story of Jesus turns into a teaching that might seem orthodox and Bible-based. This view, in fact, leaves out major parts of the story.

It is sadly possible to tick all the "correct" doctrinal and ethical boxes, to learn to pronounce all the shibboleths, but to put them all within the wrong controlling narrative—like a child who manages to join up all the dots in a follow-the-dots picture but produces a donkey instead of an elephant. Precisely because, in the world of the Enlightenment, abstract doctrines and rules have often predominated over narratives (despite the fact that the Bible itself would suggest that it should be the other way round), the church has often simply not noticed that you can affirm the Trinity, the incarnation, the atonement, the resurrection, the call to bodily holiness, and still work within a narrative which colludes with Gnosticism.[45]

Time to take off the glasses we are wearing and replace them with something better. The way we think really changes the way we approach life. "Get the gospel right, and everything else will come right."[46]

This is the Gospel

The Gospel: God becomes King on earth. He rules not through stricter rules or enforcing them better but through renewed hearts and lives of love.

THE gospel. The center of our proclamation. The Good News. Tom calls us to check whether we have got the core right. In his opinion, we have shortchanged the message for a less powerful version. He writes:

> *When people talk about preaching the gospel, they regularly mean explaining to people how they can become Christians, or perhaps explaining what it means that Christ died for their sins, or indeed telling people how to be sure of going to heaven. All of that, of course, is important. But it is not the good news, the thing itself. In particular, the church has latched onto a way of speaking about the gospel that goes like this: you are a sinner, deserving death; Jesus died in your place; therefore believe in him, and you'll go to heaven after all. This can be shortened even further to something like, Jesus took my punishment.*[47]

This version can be heard in churches the world over. It is simple, it calls for action, and it remains true. Yet, it is incomplete. We put to people the message about a legal status, with nothing for them to do but to say yes (out of nervousness for any human activity in the process) and tell them their destiny is some other place. No wonder Western Christianity struggles with discipleship (as some call it, "we are in the midst of a discipleship crisis in the Western church"[48]). Ministry to the poor, community extending into Monday through Friday, the gifts of the spirit in the body of believers, and engagement in mission—most churches struggle with these. Well, if the gospel features only part of the story, you get only part of the outworking of the Gospel.

What, then, is the gospel? Tom puts a story to us:

> *The good news is that the one true God has now taken charge of the world, in and through Jesus and his death and resurrection. The ancient hopes have indeed been fulfilled, but in a way nobody imagined. God's plan to put the world right has finally been launched. He has grasped the world in a new way, to sort it out and fill it with his glory and justice, as he always promised. But he has done so in a way beyond the wildest dreams of prophecy. The ancient*

sickness that had crippled the whole world, and humans with it, has been cured at last, so that new life can rise up in its place. Life has come to life and is pouring out like a mighty river into the world, in the form of a new power, the power of love. The good news was, and is, that all this has happened in and through Jesus; that one day it will happen, completely and utterly, to all creation; and that we humans, every single one of us, whoever we are, can be caught up in that transformation here and now. This is the Christian gospel.[49]

In Jesus, God became King. This is the news that separated the ages. This is the news that calls people to missions. This is the announcement that shakes the earth. New creation through Jesus.

We are God's images, just as in creation, and still God's partner in this world

We picked on the idea of running the world as God's partner earlier. The original creation featured this idea: God created and then handed over the keys to humans to run the show. From naming the animals to shaping the layout of the world, we co-create under God's commission. We are his images and reflect his character into the world—or not.

"Jesus's resurrection is the beginning of god's new project," says Tom, "not to snatch people away from earth to heaven but to colonize earth with the life of heaven. That, after all, is what the Lord's Prayer is about."[50]

The hope of our lives empowers us to live a life of engagement in the here and now. We are raised to new life in order to bring healing and justice to this world. We are redeemed as God's workmanship. Our hope turns to the renewal of all things. We will take up the original mandate again: to care for creation as God's stewards. To live as his image, spreading his wisdom and care to the world.

It is time to reflect on how this will play out in our lives…

How to announce God's rule

The message of Jesus: the world is under new management.

TOM introduces to us an illustration to help us grasp our current dynamic. Consider a series of shops, where one of them is taped off, a sign "under new management," The old business moved out and a new tenant took up the rights to run this place. He now designs the layout, runs the daily operations, and calls the shots. This compares to our reality as Jesus became King of the world.

The world is under new management. The King has come and is taking charge of the world. Just like a building with a sign of new ownership, so the announcement of Jesus as Lord tells everyone that someone new is now taking responsibility. Someone new runs the show from now on.

How does this new management take form in our lives? How will our cities know that a new boss has come to town? Tom suggests five key ways to live out this new time.

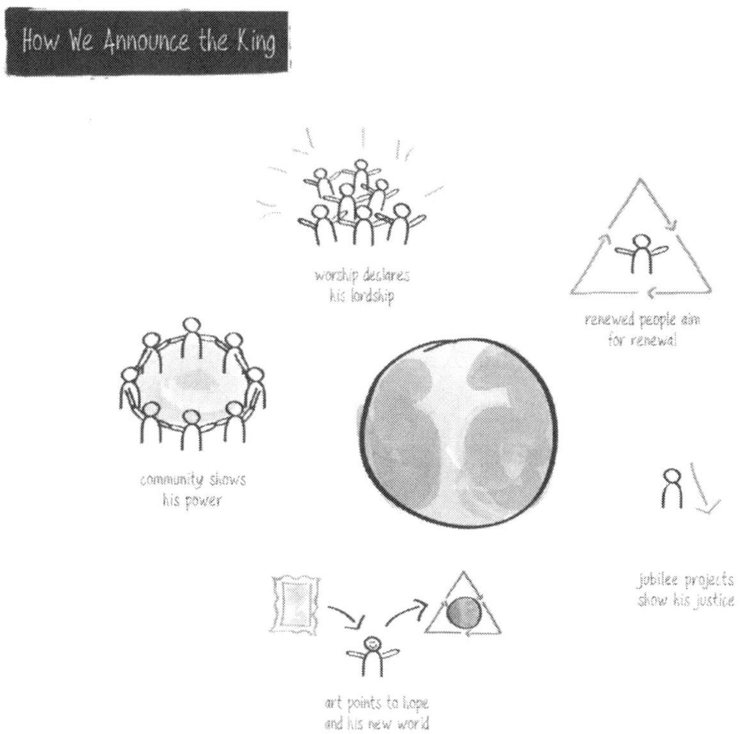

The five ways we announce God's rule in our world. These signs are noticeable from Auckland to Anchorage.

Worship, community, renewed humanity, art, and Jubilee projects. We shall turn to these now...

Worship and evangelizing

To evangelize is to announce Jesus as Lord. It differs from two lower alternatives: presenting Jesus as a better spiritual option or finding a way to avoid hell.

WORSHIP might be one of the most political acts in which we engage. Worship declares Jesus as Lord of the world. Worship undercuts other nominees. Declaring Jesus as the King of the world is a confrontation to all other king-claims, be they political rulers, be they materialism, or be they ideologies. As we declare Jesus and no other, we confront power-claims. We pledge allegiance to Jesus and follow his directions.

In worship, we celebrate the lordship of Jesus and declare it to the world. We let our hopes and ambitions be shaped by a new agenda. We commit to a new social order, to care for the pure, to holiness, and to a community that, "*marches to a different beat, that keeps in step with a different Lord.*"[51]

The proclamation of Jesus, declaring Jesus as the ruler of the world, stands at the core of our calling. Worship and evangelism go hand in hand. Both declare the kingship of Jesus.

In the history of Christianity, evangelism got a bit tilted, according to Tom. We either focused on hell and the good news of how Jesus found a way out for us, or we put better options in front of people: Jesus gives you a better life, washes you clean, gives you *real* happiness. While all of these might be true, they are only aspects of the Good News.

> *Paul's message was … about how the one true God was changing it, radically and forever. One can debate the merits of a religion, moral system, or philosophy, but a news event is discussed in a different way. Either the event happened or it didn't; if it did happen, either it means what people say it means or it doesn't. [Paul] was announcing that a world-changing event has happened.*[52]

Declaring God as Creator and Jesus as Lord over all changed the world once. Can it change the world again? It surely can. Time to pick it up again. By words and by deeds.

It should not surprise us that the key symbol in Jesus' life and teaching was a party. From the wedding banquet to the last supper, in the sharing of meals and inclusion at the table, Jesus embodied his invitation. From the invitation to Zacchaeus, to the meals at Simon's house, the teachings on the King's banquet, the breaking of bread on the road to Emmaus, and the sharing of fish with Peter, Jesus centered his symbols on coming together at the table of fellowship. All are invited. All are to share. Join the party.

The deeds matched the words. Jesus in the center brings the world together. This is our message.

Communities as a sign of God's design

reconciliation

embodying
new humanity, new world

Reconciliation embodies the new humanity. It is the sign of God's new world. Nothing could be more at the center of how God acts, and his people can take this into all the world.

THE second key sign of the kingdom comes in communities of faith. This new world happens as people are called to God's fellowship and empowered by the Spirit. They are commissioned to bring the kingdom of God into the entire world. We show the world how the world is supposed to be. We foreshadow the eventual creation. Churches and Christian groups demonstrate the nature of the King by the way they live and treat each other. The great Christ hymn in Philippians 2 links the way of Jesus with the way we are living—united and full of self-giving love. There is a new way of life open that mandates a new way to order life for Jesus' followers.

The key lies in the community of the faithful. The church stands at the core of the biblical worldview. Unity marks the people of God, and drives the mission of God. The *ekklessia* embodies the idea of the New Testament of reconciliation.

Tom says: "*The unity of the church is the sign to the powers of what God is actually all about.*"[53] It shows more than anything else how the worldview of people has changed. Tom calls the unity of the church "the central world-view symbol"[54] of the theology of Paul. The church acts as a particular kind of location and works to spread wisdom and healing.

The victory of God in Jesus creates a new entity. We are called into a body. Church is precisely not optional. Church is the sign of the new way of life. This flows from all Jesus did. From Jesus' life, the church is birthed to spread God's image around the world. This is our mission.

Art opens our eyes

Art can be a sign of hope, pointing us to how things should be. However, it frequently drifts to two lower alternatives: kitsch and sentimentalism (beauty without truth) or brutalism (truth without beauty).

THE deepest longings and conflicts of a society are picked up in art. Great art makes us see. It moves us beyond ourselves. Tom calls Christians to engage in art to shape the world. "We need to learn to imagine a world without evil and then think through the steps on how to get there."[55] Once people get a vision of what might be, they are more drawn to act.

> *The Christian imagination—shrunken and starved by the long winter of secularism—needs to be awakened, enlivened and pointed in the right direction ... thinking ahead into God's new world and into such fresh forms of*

> *worship and service as will model and embody aspects of it. We need to have this imagination energized, fed and nourished, so that it is lively and inventive.*[56]

Art can be a signpost to the new world. Like a movie trailer, a preview of the age to come, and how things are meant to be. It can fill our imagination with a vision of a better world. Therefore, art needs to be disciplined, focused, and created with a mission. This will send a message into a world that cannot come up with answers in its own arts.

Whether poetry or paintings, music or architecture, photography or calligraphy, art taps into the deepest areas of who we are, and if we connect that to the great story of God, we are agents of the kingdom of God.

We can invite art back into the center of our calling as Christians. Art can hold things together that logic needs to feed you step by step. Art can shape the way we communicate, the way we learn, and the way we celebrate. We can support artists and make space for this gift of God. Artistry belongs to our calling as images of God.

Justice implements the work of Christ

The world is in grave economic injustice. The idea of Jubilee should address this.

FINALLY, we come to Jubilee projects. Jesus announced in Luke 4, "The time has come, this is the time of Jubilee." Tom takes this up and hands the message to us: take the Jubilee idea and turn it into reality in our own time: forgive debt, release the oppressed, care for creation, overcome injustice, and declare the good news. As we think about the ills of our times, we live the story of God by embodying and acting on the Jubilee idea. In doing that, we are engaging with the calling and spreading God's glory into the world.

Here I want to pick up the Jubilee idea a bit further. If this world is infected with a disease and Jesus overcomes sin and breaks its power, then we are now God's people carrying his victory into his world. So, we as Christians implement the work of Christ whenever we overcome injustice and heal the consequences of sin.

Tom calls Christians to work for justice in our times. The kingdom of God comes not by power and might but by compassion and the meek.

> *The work of the kingdom is summed up pretty well in those Beatitudes. When God wants to change the world, he doesn't send in the tanks. He sends in the meek, the mourners, those who are hungry and thirsty for God's justice, the peacemakers, and so on. Just as God's whole style reflects his generous love, sharing his rule with his human creatures ... [who] reflect in turn the same sense of vulnerable, gentle, but powerful self-giving love..*[57]

Tom points to the current imbalance in world. The Western world holds enormous riches and power. The developing world suffers under a huge debt burden. This weighs so heavily that it does not allow any development in many of those countries. As Christians, we should work toward Isaiah's visions of valleys being raised and mountains leveled. We should stand for economic justice and forgiveness. Here we see the Jubilee idea again:

> *The West still exerts an economic stranglehold over the rest of the world. Today [there is a] phenomenon of massive global debt, where the poorest countries are heavily in debt to the richest, with compound interest mounting up the way above anyone's capacity to pay ... we are able to escalate both the divide between rich and poor and the speed of that increase.*[58]

Tom warns of keeping up a permanent imbalance as "financial systems keep whole countries in unpayable debt as it is of those whose caste system keeps tens of thousands of lower-caste peoples in squalor and penury."[59] Some of the crises we see today result directly from this dynamic. Injustice leads to poor results for everyone, just like sin.

While not everyone can affect global finance structures directly, Tom asks us to consider our choices, to engage locally, and to voice our demand to politicians for a just world. Little steps, maybe. But with the right vision we might move the world.

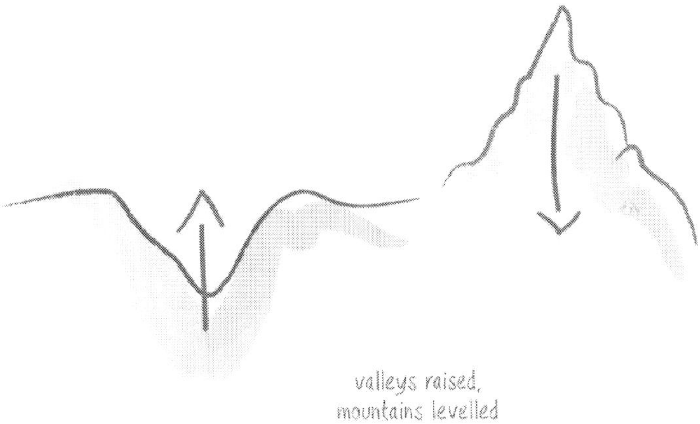

Jubilee projects fulfill Isaiah's vision of valleys raised and mountains lowered. This leveling of differences was promised as a sign of God's kingdom.

Reminding the powerful

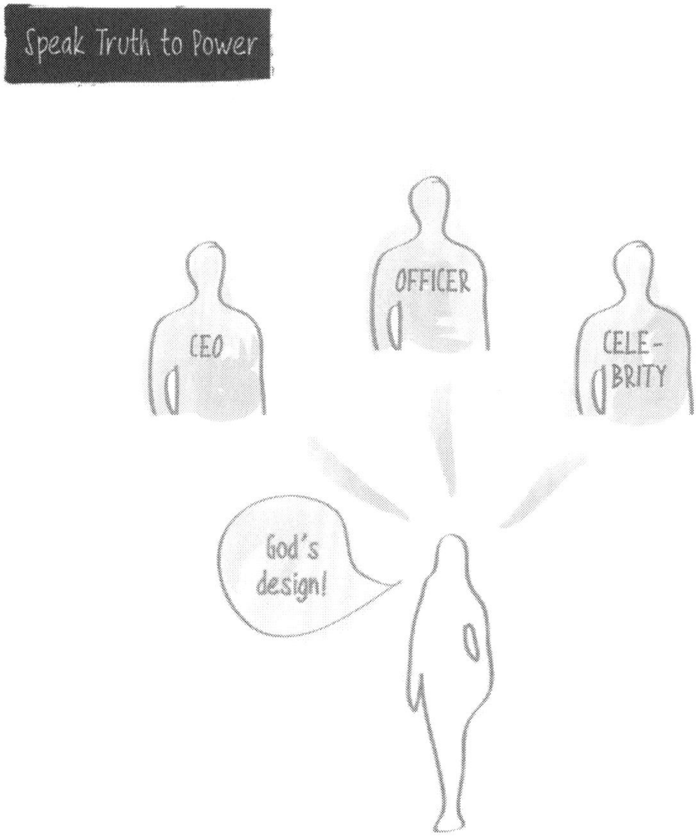

Christians are to remind those in power that they are placed there in God's wisdom and need to consider his design.

IF we are serious about this earth being under God's reign, this leads us to statements about God's role in public life. If Jesus is Lord of the world, then our faith will influence all realms of society. Much of current faith life has centered about devotions and "Christian" activities (such as prayer, evangelizing, teaching faith, small groups, etc.). This drift toward the inner life has led to an inability to put voice to our faith in the public square. Yet once we overcome the barrier in our worldview, the lordship of Jesus should speak to all institutions and organizations. Tom comments:

> *Part of the way in which the church will do this is by getting on with and setting forward those works of justice and mercy, of beauty and relationship, which the rulers know in their bones ought to be flourishing but which they seem powerless to bring about.*[60]

This relates especially to the organizations and rules in place to keep the world spinning. Until the final day, there will be structures and people in place that run the show and don't have God's new world in mind. If the new day and age have already dawned, how do these structures and people fit into the picture? Tom reminds us of the enthronement of Jesus:

> *The result, illustrated in Colossians 1:18-20, is that the rulers are reconciled—in some strange sense reinstated as the bringers of God's wise order to the world, whether or not they would see it like that ... the creator God uses even those rulers who do not know him personally to bring fresh order and even rescue the world. This lies behind the narrative of Acts.*[61]

Somehow God manages to use even the worldly rulers to bring about his purposes. Bringing the kingdom of God to our cities means the church needs to "pick up the vocation to remind the rulers of their task, to speak truth to power, and to call authorities to account."[62]

While the general idea sounds good, it might easily lead to the sort of sneering and shouting matches that are often seen as an embarrassment for Christians. That might be one of the ways for the world to shrug off unwelcome (and incomprehensible) reminders of what it should do. Wisdom is require in order for us to be agents of the Spirit's work and to "prove the world wrong on three counts: sin, justice, and judgment" (John 16:8).

Tom advises us to take this road by "providing such a wonderful model of God's genuine humanity that the world is seen as sordid and shabby in contrast."[63] The church should remind the world about justice and where they get it wrong ("favoring the rich and powerful, turning a blind eye to wickedness in high places, forgetting the cry of the poor and needy, who the Bible insists are the special objects of God's just and right care."[64]) Care for the poor is a core calling of the church, and needs to be put to those in power as a reminder and call to action.

The world runs on control and violence. The church stands to remind the world of the judgment of God—overcoming death with the power of love. Violence and death are one way the world likes to control and set boundaries. While force might be useful in some cases, it seldom solves the problems it tries to address. As Christians, we need to critique the lust for power and live a life of self-giving love by the power of the Spirit.

With all this, we remind Caesar that God's kingdom did not originate in this world. We do not impose God's rule from above, we do not shout louder than all others from the sidelines. We get involved and prototype the world to come right here in the midst of everything going on. We remind everyone with authority that they are called as stewards of God's creation.

Part Four. Living in God's New World

Four echoes in our souls

IN this last part, we move to how the message of Jesus connects to the longing of the people around us. Not everyone takes the journey through the Old Testament and what Jesus means. But everyone hears their heart speaking to them. Tom has some ideas about how that plays into the Big Story.

Then we will look to the final frame of the picture of the Bible: how we will all end up, as well as what life after death means. Finally, we will come full circle to show how we know that what we do is not done in vain.

Ready to connect some longings?

How are we led through life?

What Do We Follow

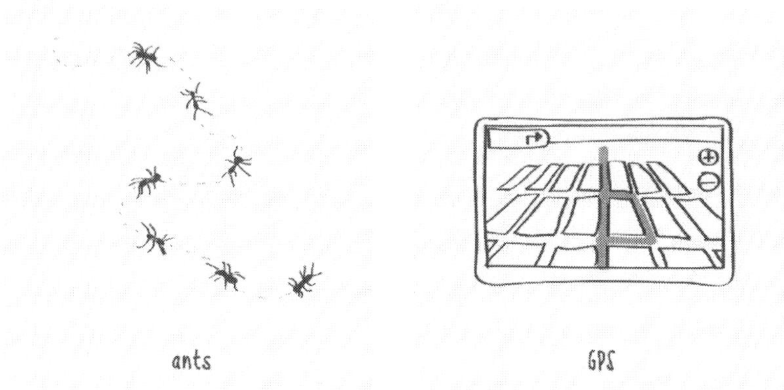

Here are two options for how we follow directions. Like the ant, we may follow the ones around us. Or like the GPS, we may be constantly redirecting ourselves toward the destiny.

From where do we get our direction for life? Tom poses that question as he analyzes culture and where we are headed as people. We all follow something. It may be those around us, some philosophy or teaching, or some inner feeling-insight mix that shapes our path in life. Tom shares an illustration of an ant with us:

> *There is a certain kind of ant which, when it's lost, is programmed to follow the ant in front. This normally works fine, because ants are pretty smart and someone up ahead will surely know where we're all going. But sometimes the ones up ahead will start to circle round, looking for another ant to follow and another, and another. And before too long all the ants will be going round and*

> *round, convinced they are marching in the right direction but all merely following one another in a great circle. And the result is catastrophic.*[65]

Tom's picture of ants following each other speaks to much of our society. The people of Israel knew an alternative: they followed a signal from outside (like a GPS) that redirected them depending on where they found themselves.

With this, Tom leads in to a discussion of various signals that we get in our hearts and minds that try to reconnect us to our path. He points to a voice that we resonate with, even though we might not know the exact source. Tom calls this "echoes of a voice."

In the next section, we explore the four echoes of this voice. We all know these echoes. They indicate that there must be something beyond us. The echoes in themselves are not enough to lead us to God. They act as strange signposts pointing us beyond. Let's look at the first one...

Longing for justice

We all want fairness. Starting at an early age, we long for justice. This is the first echo. We have three options for how to respond: we may think of it as a dream that won't ever happen; we may think of it as pointing to another reality; or we may try to identify the voice behind the echo.

THE longing for justice starts Tom's storyline of how humans are wired to receive signals from God. This echo resonates with something, and yet remains ever incomplete.

The search for justice can be seen from an early age. Kids playing with each other start wrestling about toys and call for justice. Later, we question a referee's decision in sports, or a teacher's grading, or a parent's choices. Then, we look into the wider world and find companies and countries not acting fair. Movies portray many stories of utter unfairness—and we find it in our own relationships as well. The search for justice and fairness presents itself all around.

And yet, it slips through our fingers. No matter how educated, how democratic, or how compliant we are, the sense that justice has not arrived in the world remains as clear as ever. Maybe it never will arrive.

We hear the echo of a voice. Tom proposes three options for dealing with this desired-yet-failing dynamic. One would be to become a cynic. It's all just a dream. There is no substance to it. Young, inexperienced folks might be looking for justice. The older you get, the more you see how justice remains a dream. And you better wake up to deal with reality. Option One turns cynic and laughs at the echo.

Option Two gives you an escapist vision. Well, if the longing for justice is planted in everyone, but no one seems to know how to get it, then maybe it is meant for another world. Maybe we have to simply endure the injustice here and hope that we get to the next level sometime soon. That will solve the problem. Option Two leads us into dreamland, where we hope for utopia.

The third option sees the longing and lack of fulfillment as a voice from somewhere else. Someone speaks to us. An image reflects in us. That's why we have this undeniable longing. It is meant for this world, but the voice has to add something to make it happen.

> *The Christian story claims to be the true story about God and the world. As such, it offers itself as the explanation of the voice whose echo we hear in the search for justice, the quest for spirituality, the longing for relationship, the yearning for beauty. None of these by itself points directly to God—to any God, let alone the Christian God. At best, they wave their arms in a rather general direction, like someone in a cave who hears an echoing voice but has no idea where it is coming from.*[66]

We hear the voice, somehow. It sets us up to connect with someone. The missing piece is in finding that someone and seeing how he speaks to that longing.

And we long for more in this world than justice...

Longing for beauty

incomplete masterpiece

The second echo is the desire for beauty. Beauty draws us in, but is fleeting, like an incomplete piece of a great master. Something is there that touches us, and yet, we long for something more.

Each soul connects with beauty. When we encounter a sunset, a beautiful scene, or symmetry in unexpected places, we marvel. Time slows and we remain in this place for a while. Instagram is filled with the desire to capture and remember these encounters. And yet they are fleeting.

Tom shares an illustration, a story of rummaging around an attic and discovering some scribbles on a piece of paper. It looks old, and seems like it might be music. Upon closer inspection, it appears to be a piece for piano. When it is played, it is stunning. Beautiful music.

And yet, the full score cannot be found. The piece turns out to be incomplete. There are indications that other instruments play along, but that score is missing. The piece might be from Mozart, as of yet undiscovered and a witness to a great genius. Breathtaking, yet incomplete.

Beauty touches something in us. It satisfies. And yet we cannot contain it. "Satisfied, yet longing." Beauty points to a voice beyond. Something that every person longs for. Something that every person understands. And something that no one can fully grasp or contain.

Building on justice and beauty, there is a human element we cannot quite grasp…

Craving connection

The third echo is the search for connection. It started in the Garden with God's calling of Adam. Connection is rooted in the Trinity.

THE longing for relationship echoes to all people the world over. Even introverts want and need connection, someone to know, and someone to be known to. From an early age, we associate, we explore, we bond. We are made for each other. If relationships go well, we feel fully human. We know instinctively that we belong to a larger scheme of things.

The longing for company points to the Bible's opening. There, man is created in the image of God, and it is said that "it is not good that man is alone." And so God creates companionship for him.

A little later, the voice of God goes out into the world: "Adam, where are you?" God himself seeks connection. We carry this deep within us. It reflects the Trinity.

However, this longing also remains frustrated. While we do find others with whom to connect, most relationships are a mix of joy and sorrow, of blessing and bleeding. We arrange ourselves with some mid-level mix of connecting on some levels and remaining lonely on others:

> *We all know that we belong in communities, that we were made to be social creatures. Yet there are many times when we are tempted to slam the door and stomp off into the night by ourselves, simultaneously making the statement that we don't belong any more and that we want someone to take pity on us, to come to the rescue and comfort us. We all know we belong in relationships, but we can't quite work out how to get them right.*[67]

The echo needs a voice with which to connect. Someone has to step into our world to keep us from turning cynic or escapist.

The final echo makes us look for the voice the most…

Searching for meaning

springs

concrete

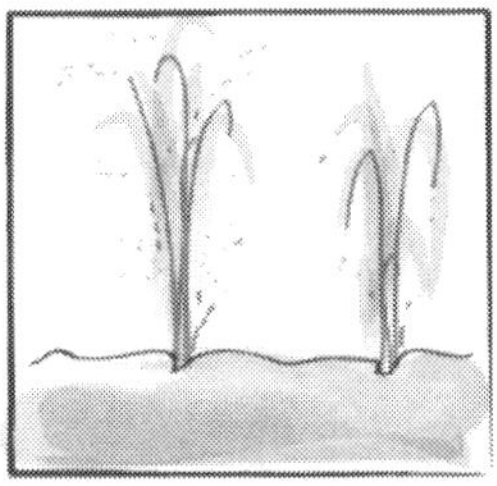

breaking forth

The fourth echo is the quest for spirituality. It is like a land where the spring flows freely—everyone longs for higher meaning. Western rationalism tries to plaster over it and keep it contained, but it keeps bubbling up all over. We need meaning and purpose.

IMAGINE a country where all over the place springs burst forth and flood the country with fresh water.. Then, a ruler wants to impose some order and firm up the ground. He has the ground flattened and poured over with concrete. What once was a pool of fresh water is now turned into a functional space with clear corners.

This remains as it is for a decade or two. Underneath the surface, the springs have been continuing to pour out, increasing in strength. Then, one day, a spring bursts through the concrete. The officials rush to fix it and keep the unwanted water out. Soon, another spot breaks in the concrete. Then, another. Until all over the country the springs are breaking their way through the official's desire to keep them out.

Our desire for spirituality acts like that. We search for meaning. We want a larger story to which to connect our lives. While our culture wants science to replace religion, and the public discourse shuns emotional and spiritual explanations, the longing for meaning can't be contained. Spirituality is the hidden spring that bubbles in human hearts. The longing for sense, the longing for something beyond numbers and formulas, stirs deeply in the human nature. The echo of a voice.

Which leads us to the way to connect all of these echoes…

Heaven and earth will marry

Three options for how God relates to us

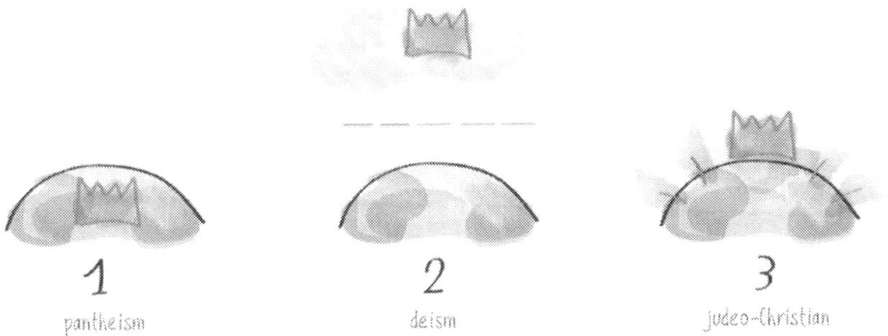

There are three options for how God relates to our world. Pantheism sees God in everything. Deism sees God as far away and split from our reality. The Jews and Christians see God as separate, but interlocking with our reality.

ALL of this incompleteness sounds a bit depressing. So, well, wishful. And what are we to make of it? If most things in life leave us yearning and feeling they are outside our reach, how are we to deal with it? Cynicism and escapism sound like real alternatives—and it is understandable why people would take this route.

Once you take a closer look at what lies behind these options, things might clear up a bit. Tom gives us three ways to look at it in the chapter "God" in *Simply Christian*. He asks us to consider how God is related to our world.

Option 1 is God in everything. The school of pantheism spells this out. Stoicism is one school of this type. Matter and things are shot through with God. While this might sound attractive to some, it has trouble dealing with evil and does not have many adherents these days. In older cultures, people sacrificed and read the signs of weather and fate to find a peaceful way with the God-in-everything dynamic. Our modern materialism has pushed this option out of the minds of most people.

Option 2 separates God from human affairs. This is basically the deist vision (and what comes up as *Epicureanism* in Tom's writing). There exists a gulf between us and God. The world runs on natural laws and the consequences of human action. This seems to be the most common idea in today's world, both in culture at large and within the church.

These two options feed the cynic and escapist tendencies in dealing with the echoes. Either we call those four echoes silly jokes and turn cynic or we figure earth is not the place to find any fulfillment, so we are left yearning for an afterlife. If relationships remain incomplete, it is time to lower our expectations or utilize them to the best we can. And so the story goes.

However, the third option might be the best way forward. The Jewish understanding of God's relationship to the world picked up an entirely different dynamic—heaven and earth connect. They are not separate, but touch in many ways.

> *For the ancient Israelite, and the early Christian, the creation of the world was the free outpouring of God's powerful love. The one true God made a world and has remained in a close, dynamic and intimate relationship with it, without in any way being contained within it or having it contained within himself.*[68]

God remains connected to his creation. Heaven is God's dimension to reality, while earth is man's. They overlap and interlock. The temple is the place where heaven and earth met. As we have seen, Jesus relates that to himself and promises his Spirit as God-in-action for everyone. Paul calls Christians the temples of God. Heaven and earth touching.

Within this third option, the echoes connect us to the voice. Justice comes with God's action and in his judgment, setting everything right. For beauty we see it as a sign pointing us forward: "All the beauty of the present world will be enhanced, ennobled, set free from that which at present corrupts and defaces it. Then there will appear that greater beauty for which the beauty we already know is simply an advance signpost."[69] Through the Spirit, we are offered a new form of relationships with our neighbors and all of creation. Our quest for spirituality is answered by the coming together of heaven and earth, when we find our purpose in God's creation.

The echoes find their answers in the act of God in Jesus. As Jesus brought heaven and earth together, we get to experience the Person speaking whose echo we heard.

Interlocking of heaven and earth

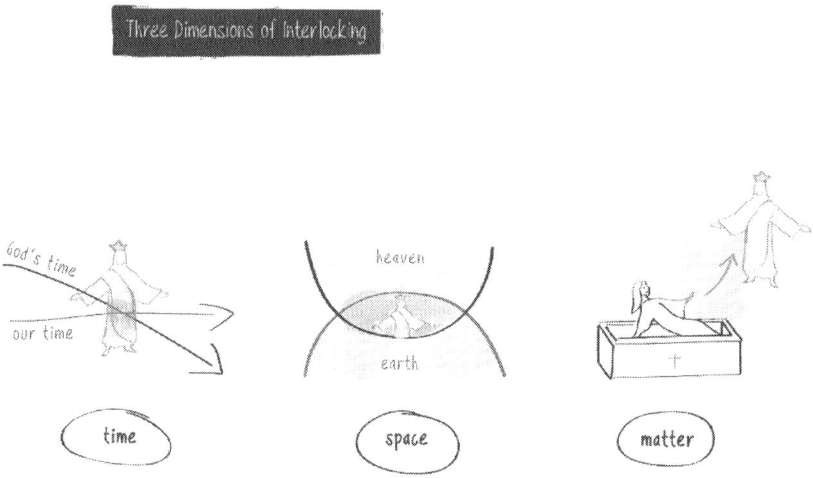

Heaven and earth interlock. Time, space, and matter are the three dimensions within which we live our lives. The Bible tells the story of how in Jesus heaven came to interlock with time, space, and matter.

It is time to pick up the earlier idea of overlapping dimensions. What happens in time, space, and matter shows how heaven and earth will connect from now on. Jesus triggered this overlap, and we get to enjoy it from this point forward:

> *God's time and ours overlap and intersect, God's space and ours overlap and interlock, and even (this is the really startling one, of course) the sheer material world of God's creation is infused, suffused, and flooded with God's own life and love and glory.*[70]

This speaks to the intent and purpose of God, which was filling the earth with his glory. If we see a great gulf between earth and heaven, we miss the dynamic. Once we see how heaven and earth are connected, the life of heaven becomes much more real. Heaven is linked to our lives—and we don't have to wait until after Armageddon. God planned to fully link heaven and earth, to be all in all, to *"fill the world with his glory and love, to transform everything, to rectify everything, to heal everything with his powerful love."*[71]

We truly live between the times. Something has started: heaven touches earth already, and this puts the taste of the final joining of heaven and earth in our mouths. What God did in Jesus, he will do one day for all.

Jesus came to heal. Jesus came to save. Jesus came to judge. And one day that will be for everything…

How the movie ends

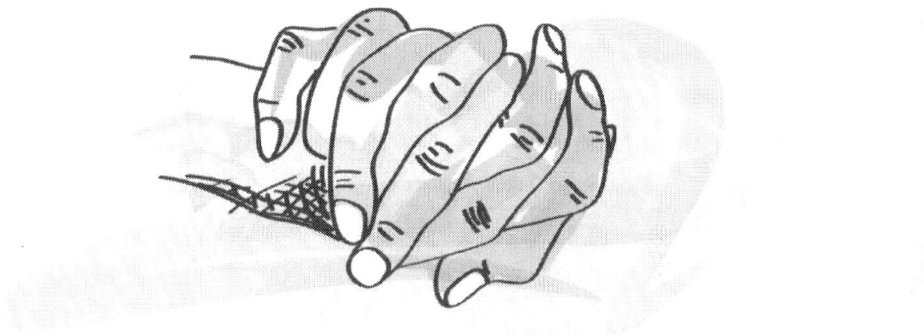

Joined together—the final frame in the Bible's story. Heaven and earth finally are joined fully.

EVERY movie ends with a frame. Tom reminds us loud and clear that the Bible comes as a story. We are to be part of that story. And we know how the story ends. Revelations 21shows us the final frame of our story:

> *Heaven, in the Bible, is not a future destiny but the other, hidden, dimension of our ordinary life—God's dimension, if you like. God made heaven and earth; at the last he will remake both and join them together forever. And when we come to the picture of the actual end in Revelation 21–22, we find not ransomed souls making their way to a disembodied heaven but rather the new Jerusalem coming down from heaven to earth, uniting the two in a lasting embrace.*[72]

The marriage of heaven and earth—the conclusion of history.

> *The goal of that whole project is sketched in Revelation 21 and 22. The God of the Bible is not in the business either of abandoning or of destroying his creation.... The heart of early Christianity was the belief that in Jesus of Nazareth the creator God had dealt with the rebellion and corruption of the present creation, particularly of the humans who were supposed to be in charge of it, and had opened up the new and living way into a new and living creation in which the original intention would now be fulfilled.*[73]

Look at what is going on. Heaven is finally joined to earth. They fully overlap now. God's sphere and ours have been brought together.

Connecting Heaven and Earth

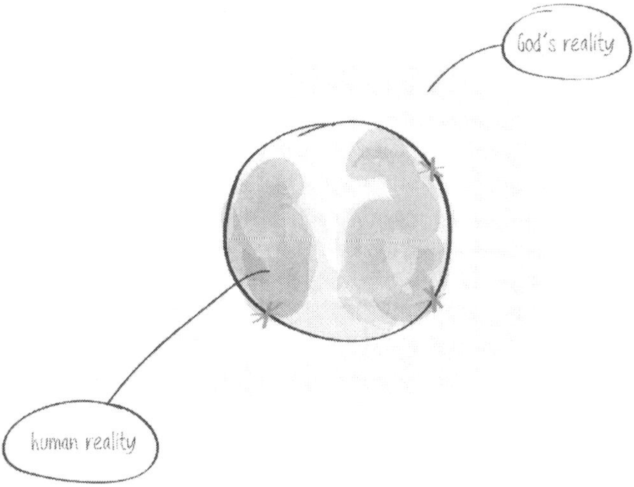

Earth is our reality, while heaven is God's dimension of that reality. The message of the Bible is the touch and interlock of those two dimensions. One day that interlock will be fully and finally completed.

We wait for this final act of God. We are sure of it because of what happened in Jesus. We experience some aspects of it already. This powers our hope going forward.

This is life after death: The dead will rise, and the earth will be as intended

Confused views on hope

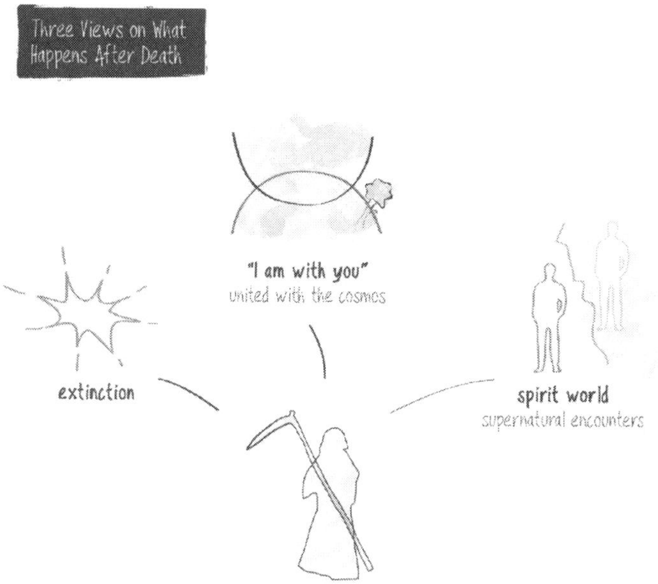

The modern view on death: either a complete end of life, a romantic merger with everything, or a spirit world. This is more informed by Hollywood than by any serious thinking.

TOM'S biggest seller is entitled, "Surprised by Hope." The book covers life after death and how the world will end. He looks at the hope that fuels our days and drives us forward. Hope makes the world tick, and forms a central aspect of the Christian worldview. Yet both the world and the main-line Christians are wrong in their hope, says Tom.

Let's start with the world. The secular person of our day has hardly developed any view of ultimate destiny. There are three usual responses to the question of what life-after-death may be like. The first one is that souls will simply cease to exist. Annihilation. Game over. Nothing. The second response considers some version of "souls in transit"—the dead somehow float through matter and show themselves from time to time. This seems heavily informed by Hollywood and defies any real connection to time and space. The third option looks at some sort of merging with everything else. "I am with you always" seems to be the sketchy refrain of this theory, and somehow the dead hang around. Their eyes are watching over us.

There is no one clear view held by most people in the world.

Most Christians these days hold a view that is similar: the dead souls will be swept up and move toward "a light" (associated with God). The souls will float in a ghost-like fashion and leave the earth for some sort of paradise. The New Jerusalem awaits—usually in a place very different from this current reality.

Saved from or saved for? Many people assume the world is a dark and decayed place to be rescued from. The New Testament says that we are saved for something—to live a life of God's design in this world.

That doesn't match the Bible, says Tom. "The reign of God's restorative justice and healing peace is meant for this world, not for some other."[74]

Somehow our Christian imagination has been primed to assume the earth busting apart and Christians finding a blissful world that matches our dreams. The idea that this world will go on (renewed, that is) stuns people. Arguing that there will be a New York City in the new world comes across like asking people to do a Bible study on cucumbers. Totally off the map.

Let us look at three reasons why the world might be very this-worldly (and contain a new New York City): one, God created the world and called it good. The prophecies are for the "knowledge of God to cover the earth as the water covers the sea" (Hab. 2:14). There are many promises to not destroy the world anymore (as in Noah) and to let it stand firm.

Two, we are taught to pray for God's reign on earth. How very strange: we pray for the span of our lives for God's kingdom on earth—and then supposedly he turns around and tells us, "Nice try, but I really meant some other place where the kingdom finally goes". The story moves toward the new Jerusalem coming to earth.

Three, God runs a redeeming business. Jesus came to redeem people and to redeem the world. Paul points us to the fact that the "creation waits in eager expectation for God's children to be revealed ... so that the bondage to decay will cease" (Rom 8.19–21). If God redeems things, how come our mental picture is of him as the Great Destroyer? Nothing is beyond his reach.

Tom gives us another great illustration:

> *It is as though you were to get a letter from the president of the United States inviting himself to stay at your home, and in your excitement you misread it and assumed that he was inviting you to stay at the White House.*[75]

We got hope wrong. When we wait for the world to pass, we are waiting for the wrong thing. The Bible sets out the renewal of God's good creation. We better join the movement.

Direction Matters

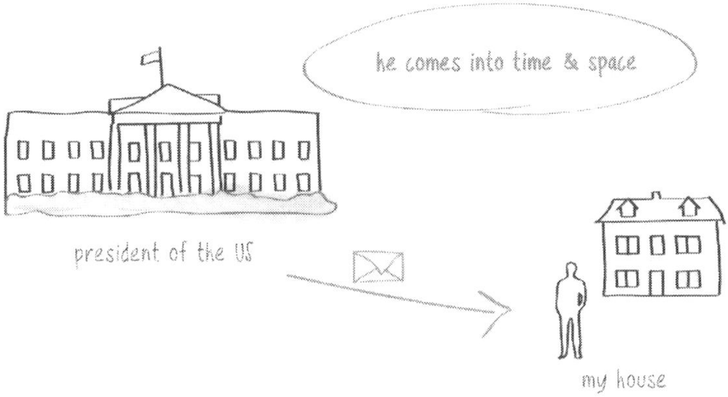

Imagine the president of the United States wanting to visit you, and in your excitement you journey to the White House. Who visits who actually matters. God came to the earth—and will return again.

Let us now look at our own lives and where we end up…

Life after life after death

There are two steps in life after death: waiting in the garden (sometimes called paradise), and then the resurrection of the bodies to new life.

SO what, then, is the biblical Christian hope? Tom wrote a book on this (*Surprised by Hope*), and his key idea is this:

> *The early Christians hold firmly to a two-step belief about the future: first, death and whatever lies immediately beyond; second, a new bodily existence in a newly remade world.*[76]

The idea of life after death remains incomplete, in Tom's view. After death comes the intermediate period—what some call paradise, or the garden, or sleeping. How this exactly happens and who ends up where is not clear.

We do know that there will be a "day of the Lord" that will consume all things. This is the second coming of Jesus. At that time, the dead will rise with a physical body. Which age, which shape, and which exact features the dead will have at this time are never discussed, but it is believed that they will be somewhat similar to normal life. Just look at Jesus—he was not running around like Godzilla or with angel's wings. He was mistaken for a Gardener or some other fellow. He ate, he had hands with marks on them, and so on.

Furthermore, this resurrection will take place on this planet. There will be the Hudson River and the Alps. The planet will go on. Just like our bodies, it will be similar and renewed. Freed from the bondage. Creation itself will experience an Exodus and return home from exile.

The churches of the New Testament certainly didn't expect the time-space universe to blow to pieces. Paul warned the church not to take letters or information from others as meaning that the final day was here:

We ask you, brothers and sisters, not to become easily unsettled or alarmed by the teaching allegedly from us—whether by a prophecy or by word of mouth or by letter—asserting that the day of the Lord has already come. (2 Thess. 2:2)

Resurrected bodies on the cleaned-up planet Earth. This is life after life after death.

Like a trailer of the future

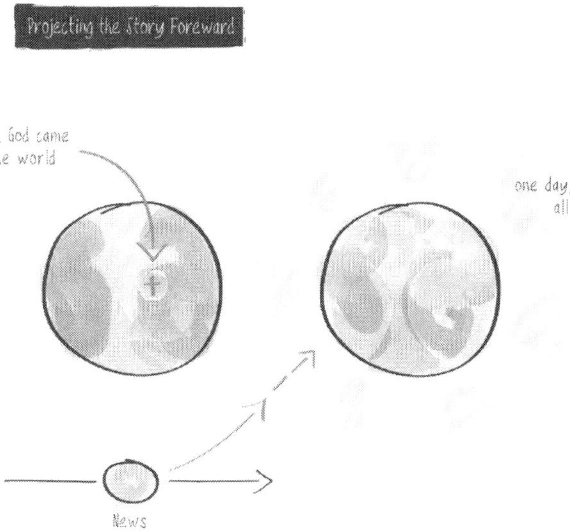

Why is the resurrection of Jesus such big news? What he started in Jesus will be true for all the world. In Jesus, the renewal has started. What happened with him will one day happen to everything.

WHAT will the cleaned-up world look like? We are reminded of the poetic prophecies of the Psalms and Isaiah. We look into the apocalyptic writing of Daniel and Revelations. And we read the pointers in the Gospels and in Paul. The fact remains: we don't really know a whole lot of details. It will be different, and it will be similar. Jesus' life and actions point to our final destiny. What God did in Jesus, he will do to the whole world. The presence of God will be everywhere.

The creational vibe can be seen in many sections across the Bible. Isaiah and the Psalms, Jeremiah and Amos speak in vivid language of the "Day of the Lord." The setting right of things and the coming of God makes creation leap for joy. They all join: the mountains and the rivers, the sea and the trees, the fields and the heavens.

Let the heavens rejoice, let the earth be glad;
let the sea resound, and all that is in it.
Let the fields be jubilant, and everything in them;
let all the trees of the forest sing for joy.
Let all creation rejoice before the Lord, for he comes,
he comes to judge the earth.[77]

Let the sea resound, and everything in it,
the world, and all who live in it.
Let the rivers clap their hands,
let the mountains sing together for joy;[78]

And even then, when the love of God floods everything, there is an opening sequence to more progress. Just when we thought everything was clean and cut, we read the following (Rev 22:1–2):

Then the angel showed me the river of the water of life, as clear as crystal, flowing from the throne of God and of the Lamb down the middle of the great street of the city. On each side of the river stood the tree of life, bearing twelve crops of fruit, yielding its fruit every month. And the leaves of the tree are for the healing of the nations.

God filling everything will leave a place for healing. Somehow, the project remains open and ongoing. Therefore…

What we did was not in vain

Deeds will last into the future

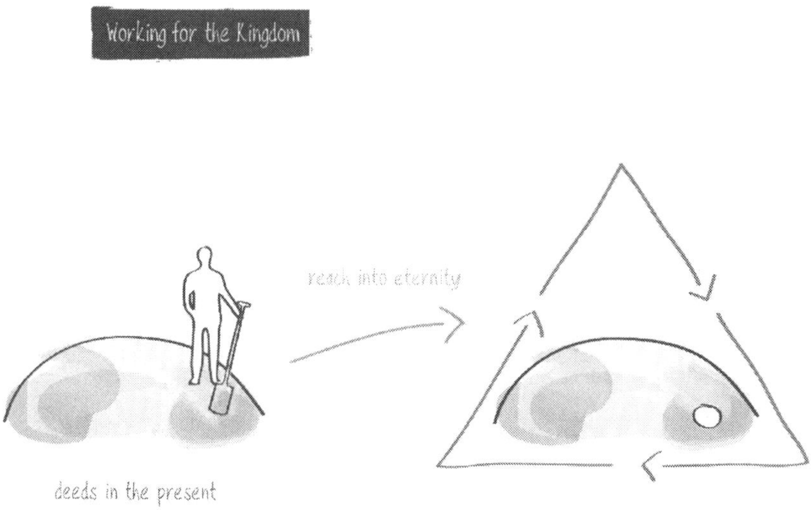

What we do now will somehow reach into eternity. Our works for the kingdom will feature in God's new world.

As Christians, we already share in the new creation. We are restored to fellowship with God, renewed in his image. As such, we live in his kingdom, reflecting his image to all of creation. Starting now. His kingdom is here. And the kingdom means collaboration all the way along. Starting now, and then going on forever.

The now-and-not yet of the kingdom gives us a task to do: reigning. Those quirky passages in 2 Timothy 2:12 or 1 Corinthians 6:2 point to a role for our lives. Humans reign as stewards in God's place. This prepares us for the time when God will be all in all and we will share his glory in caring for creation. What we learn now will enable us for our task in eternity.

The glory is not something apart from the humans involved, something at which they might be allowed to gaze.... "Rejoicing in the hope of the glory of God" (Rom 5:2) can be seen in terms of "sharing" the divine glory, but for a full understanding it is important not to short-circuit the Jewish hope and jump straight into the modern expression of "glory" as an inexact synonym for "heaven." Paul is talking about the renewal and restoration of creation, and about the role within that purpose of human beings in whom the spirit has been at work. The Messiah will "inherit" the whole world, as Psalm 2 promised.... And the Messiah's people, the full seed of Abraham, will share that inheritance, because the divine spirit has taken up residence in them to enable them to fulfill the intention which the creator had purposed, from the beginning, for his image-bearing human creatures.[79]

The judging and healing of people means being repurposed to the original idea of sharing God in the world. Even beyond learning, our task at the moment calls us to do something of value that will outlast this age.

What you do in the present—by painting, preaching, singing, sewing, praying, teaching, building hospitals, digging wells, campaigning for justice, writing poems, caring for the needy, loving your neighbour as yourself—will last into God's future. These activities are not simply ways of making the present life a little less beastly, a little more bearable, until the day when we leave it behind altogether.... They are part of what we may call building for God's kingdom.[80]

What we do here and now impacts our preparation for eternity and shapes some aspects of the future age already. That is our task. And we better get our churches aligned.

What we do is not wasted

Though a stonemason may work on a simple piece, his work will become a part of a great building. Likewise, our works here will be joined together in God's great design.

Tom points out that one of the great passages in Paul encourages us to see the link between our current deeds and God's new creation. 1 Corinthians 15 deals with the final consummation. With Jesus, we live in the new age. We are still awaiting the full consummation, though. Now and not yet. We live between the times. Like a teenager. Like the dawn of the new day. Started, but not yet complete. And 1 Corinthians 15 talks about the day when things will be complete: the new body, the overcoming of death, the final victory.

And then it goes on. First Corinthians 15:58 tells us, "Therefore, my dear brothers and sisters, stand firm. Let nothing move you. Always give yourselves fully to the work of the Lord, *because* you know that your labor in the Lord is not in vain."

Note the word: *because.* First Corinthians just spent a chapter telling us about the time after the resurrection of all people, and then: *because.* You know your labor is not in vain. What we do now links to then. Our deeds will echo into eternity. They will have a place in God's fulfilled plans. Tom reminds us, "the resurrection means that what you do in the present, in working hard for the gospel, is not wasted. It is not in vain. It will be completed, will have its fulfillment, in God's future."[81] This changes the motivation and engagement in our world:

> *You are not oiling the wheels of a machine that's about to roll over a cliff. You are not restoring a great painting that's shortly going to be thrown on the fire. You are not planting roses in a garden that's about to be dug up for a building site. You are accomplishing something that will become in due course part of God's new world. Every act of love, gratitude, and kindness; every work of art or music inspired by the love of God and delight in the beauty of his creation; every minute spent teaching a severely handicapped child to read or to walk; every act of care and nurture, of comfort and support, for one's fellow human beings and for that matter one's fellow nonhuman creatures; and of course every prayer, all Spirit-led teaching, every deed that spreads the gospel, builds up the church, embraces and embodies holiness rather than corruption, and makes the name of Jesus honored in the world—all of this will find its way, through the resurrecting power of God, into the new creation that God will one day make. That is the logic of the mission of God. God's recreation of his wonderful world, which began with the resurrection of Jesus and continues mysteriously as God's people live in the risen Christ and in the power of his Spirit, means that what we do in Christ and by the Spirit in the present is not wasted. It will last all the way into God's new world. In fact, it will be enhanced there.*[82]

What we do here and now remain piecework, but the pieces will be found in the final great design. Somehow, our incomplete actions will outlast our lives here on earth. They will be put together in God's great scheme of beauty, like "the stonemason working on part of a great cathedral," says Tom.

"They are vaguely aware that the others are getting on with their tasks.... But they trust the architect that the work they have done in following instructions will not be wasted. They are not, themselves, building the cathedral, but they are building for the cathedral, and when the cathedral is complete their work will be enhanced, ennobled, will mean much more than it could have meant as they were chiseling it and shaping it down in the stonemasons' yard."[83] Tom summarizes, "build for God's kingdom. What we do in the present, as Paul insists, is not wasted (1 Cor. 15:58). It will all be part of the eventual structure, even though at the moment we have no idea how."[84] It starts today.

Jesus rearranges everything

The story of Jesus is like a magnificent picture. The whole house needs to be rearranged for it to have a proper place. Our lives need to center around the story of Jesus.

WE have come full course on our tour of Tom Wright. He once was asked what he would tell his children on his death bed. "Look at Jesus," was his answer. "The dynamism of the Gospel and the person who walks out of those pages to meet us is just central and irreplaceable. He is always a surprise. We never have Jesus in our pocket. He is always coming at us from different angles.... If you want to know who God is, look at Jesus. If you want to know what it means to be human, look at Jesus. If you want to know what love is, look at Jesus. And go on looking until you're not just a spectator, but part of a drama that has him as the central character."[85]

This message can reform our faith. It can carry the church into the next centuries. It can change the world again in our day. It can call your life into a new mode. Tom offers one more illustration to us:

> *A rich alumnus gives to a university a wonderful, glorious painting that simply won't fit any of the spaces available in the university. The painting is so magnificent that eventually the university decides to pull itself down and rebuild itself around this great and unexpected gift, discovering as it does so that all the best things about the university the way it was are enhanced within the new structure, and all the problems of which people had already been aware are thereby dealt with.*[86]

Tom paints us a picture of the Great Event that happened in Jesus. He portrays a Messiah that was well above any expectations. Once we dig into his story and the reality of what we accomplished, we understand how, "In him, and through him, and for him all things" were made. What happened in Jesus splits the ages. What he did ushered in a completely new time. God is here—and we are grateful to be alive!

Outro: Which song do you sing?

What Do We Expect?

Jesus as singer, turning our tune into a nice song

Jesus as composer, teaching us the music of a new world

The challenge of Jesus is that we want someone to sing our song, but Jesus came to teach us a completely new music. We want him as our singer, but he is the composer instead.

WE have taken a tour through one of today's greatest minds. Tom Wright speaks to us in a fresh voice. He reminds us what the central things are really all about. He calls us to read the Bible with God as the main actor, and not the self as the seeker for enlightenment. He asks us to rearrange our vision of how God deals with everything he created, ourselves included.

> *We have reduced the kingdom of God to private piety, the victory of the cross to comfort for the conscience, and Easter itself to a happy, escapist ending after*

a sad, dark tale. Piety, conscience, and ultimate happiness are important, but not nearly as important as Jesus himself.[87]

This shift of perspective can change the direction we travel in as Christians. It can change the impact we have on the world. As we refocus on God, on God's kingdom, and on God's faithfulness, we will be energized with fresh vision and empowered by the presence of the Spirit. This shift comes at a price: we are called to lay everything down before a new King. It really is about kingship. And we are all given this simple choice. Are we willing to follow?

They were looking for a builder to construct the home they thought they wanted, but he was the architect, coming with a new plan that would give them everything they needed, but within quite a new framework. They were looking for a singer to sing the song they had been humming for a long time, but he was the composer, bringing them a new song to which the old songs they knew would form, at best, the background music. He was the king, all right, but he had come to redefine kingship itself around his own work, his own mission, his own fate.[88]

Are you ready to sing the new song?

What's Next

WHAT is the kingdom of God? And how is it worked out in our time and our town? This question is at the heart of our network, Spark Europe. We look to plant churches, develop art, start social businesses and empower kingdom agents in postmodern Europe. Join our tribe

NT Wright continues to research and publish. We have set up a blog to support this book. You will find some background story on the process of this book and video summaries of Tom's past and upcoming works. Also, we have added a pack of pictures for your use to spread the message. You will find 116 pictures – some previously unpublished material on Tom's thought is available there.

Finally, there is a growing number of resources out there to dig into Tom's think. ntwrightpage.com is a comprehensive set of lectures, links and audios, and has been running since 2004. ntwrightonline.org runs world-class courses with NT Wright – both on select topics as well as studies of Bible books. The Facebook page of Tom shows many of his speaking engagements and projects. Additionally, we have added an appendix here to dig deeper on any of the chapters you wish to explore.

THE BEST IS YET TO COME!

Appendix: FAQs

No guide earns its money without addressing some key questions. This list should address the most common questions and objections to Tom's ideas.

Isn't this all too complicated?
It is like explaining to someone how to get from Germany to Italy. You can either say it simply: just go south. Or you give a bit more detailed explanation of what you will encounter. And the journey there goes through the Alps, giving you wonderful details that are in themselves breathtaking to explain.

Do we have to be historians to understand the Bible?
The Bible is written as a history book. If we ignore that fact, we are in danger of drawing false conclusions or just projecting into the story whatever we want. So, dealing with the history helps in getting the message straight. Knowing what something meant in another culture is especially important, because it helps give proper weight to the statements.

Doesn't it say that heaven and earth will dissolve?
There are numerous passages that speak of cataclysmic events. Heard with Gnostic ears, they would indicate an end of the time-space universe. However, this might say more about the assumptions that someone brings to those texts than about those texts themselves. For the Jews who were rooted in the goodness of creation and the expectation of redemption, those texts were read as apocalyptic—meaning they used dramatic language to explain large-scale events within time and space. So, if they talked about the end of the Roman Empire, they might say that the sun would melt. They did not literally mean the end of the sun, just very dramatic events – within time and space.

Did Tom kill substitutionary atonement?
No. He maintains that Jesus took our sins upon himself. He argues that he is the justice and faithfulness of God. Tom just puts that in the context of a larger story: God's dealing with creation. Tom did kill something, though: the worldview of Gnosticism in a Christian setting. He replaced it with the Jewish worldview of creation, judgment, and resurrection.

Isn't it dangerous to change the meaning of words, as Tom does?
Changing the meaning of words makes communication tricky. It happens all the time—just watch a movie from the sixties. If it happens over the course of fifty years, then it will certainly happen over the course of two thousand years. And since understanding the Bible is important, Tom questions current use of key words and seeks their original meaning. That is what scholarship and serious study is all about.

Isn't this just a fad—saying we discovered the real truth now after two thousand years of Christendom?
Every generation needs to seek to understand the Bible and its relevance to their context. Christian history is filled with attempts to work out what the events of Jesus mean. This is unfinished work and will go on.

Where are the miracles in Tom's teachings?
Tom comes at the text as a theologian with an emphasis on history. He discusses issues to tease out the underlying worldview. For him, miracles are signposts, mainly, even though he has experienced some himself. He does not teach or advocate them in the way that some churches do these days.

How can an average Joe have any hope of impacting global debt structures?
Complex issues usually need a host of approaches to tackle them. One area is politics, both national and local. Joe can make his voice heard and call politicians to their task of addressing the issues. Another area is personal projects that embody some aspect of addressing financial inequality—be it participating in some project or thinking through some aspect of the issue and pioneering new ways of addressing it.

Working for the kingdom—is Tom suggesting that it depends on human effort?
Yes, he is. Humans are designed to be stewards of God's creation. So, the efforts of humans do have real effects on his creation, as well as on other people. God has given his action plan into the hands of people. On the other hand, the final judgment and redemption is God's act. It is a partnership -with God as the senior partner.

Will the world become ever better?

No. Some things will improve. The kingdom will come more and advance. But the darkness will remain. The evil forces are present, as ever, and will not be abolished before the second coming of Jesus.

Does Tom believe in hell?

He finds it tricky territory. In *Surprised by Hope*, he talks about his own ignorance on these matters. He speaks of three options: eternal damnation, annihilation, and ongoing redemption of everyone. He leaves it open on where he stands, indicating the second option. Tom reminds us that it is not appropriate for Christians to think about who else should be punished. Also, he reminds us that the Bible is about the marriage of heaven and earth, not hell and earth. This context needs to be primary.

Appendix: Digging deeper

WE serve you some more pointers if you want to explore Tom further. These chapters or subchapters in these books, courses and videos help you explore the comprehensive thinking of Tom and dig for yourself. Part One remains somewhat open – Tom does not provide an autobiography or lengthy personal accounts.

Part TWO – What is new in Tom?

The Bible as story
We filter the story out of the mix
Webpage: How Can The Bible Be Authoritative?
http://ntwrightpage.com/Wright_Bible_Authoritative.htm

Understanding Scripture as a drama
Scripture and the Authority of God, Chapter 1: By Whose Authority?

Why Abraham
Paul and the Faithfulness of God. Chapter 10: The People of God, Freshly Revealed.

Striking a deal
Udemy, Galatians (video). Section 4, Lecture 16 - https://www.udemy.com/paul-and-his-letter-to-the-galatians/learn/v4/t/lecture/2720216

The promise fulfilled
Udemy, Galatians (video). Section 4, Lecture 18 - https://www.udemy.com/paul-and-his-letter-to-the-galatians/learn/v4/t/lecture/2720228

How will the story play out?
Creation, Power, Truth. Chapter 1 – Glimpses of Gnosis in Western Culture

The event in Jesus
How we misunderstood the Gospel
Simply Good News. Chapter 2 – The Backstory

From Personal to Private Religion
Surprised by Scripture. Chapter 7 – How the Bible Reads the Modern World.

God arrived in history
How God became King. Chapter 5: Glory Unveiled: John's Temple Christology.

Easter speaks about this world
Surprised by Hope. Chapter 4: The Strange Story of Easter.

What the Kingdom of God means

The expectation: homecoming
Jesus and the Victory of God. Chapter 13: The return of the King

The answer: new creation
Following Jesus. Chapter 4: The Glory of God: John.

The new in the middle of the old
Paul and the Faithfulness of God. Chapter 11, Section 5: God's Future for the World, Freshly Imagined / Eschatology and Christian Living.

This is the kingdom
How God became King. Chapter 10: Kingdom and Cross.

A new take on morals

Chasing happiness
After you believe. Chapter 2: The Transformation of Character. Three.

Forget happiness, you are called to a throne
Surprised by Scripture. Chapter 5: Jesus is Coming – Plant a Tree!

Creation is an open project
After you Believe. Chapter 3: Priests and Rulers.

Preparing to participate in God's project
After you believe. Chapter 2: The Transformation of Character. Eight.

Reflecting God into the world
After you believe. Chapter 7: Virtue in Action: The Royal Priesthood. Four.

Part THREE– The story changed

A new pair of eyes to see

How the mind is transformed

The Case for the Psalms. Chapter 1: Introduction.

How worldviews work

The New Testament and the People of God. Chapter 8: Story, Symbol, Praxis.

Worldview of 21st century

Udemy, Worldviews (video). Section 6, lecture 27 - https://www.udemy.com/worldviews-the-bible-and-the-believer/learn/v4/t/lecture/2837238

Worldview of Paul

Paul and the Faithfulness of God. Chapter 8: Five Signposts of the Apostolic Mindset.

Why we all think God lives upstairs

Creation, Power, Truth. Chapter 1: Against Contemporary Gnosticism

What we can't see

Surprised by Scripture. Chapter 3: What History and Science Have to Say about Easter

This is the Gospel

Simply Good News. Chapter 4: Distorted and Competing Gospels

We are God's images, just as in creation, and still God's partner in this world

How to announce God's rule

Simply Jesus. Chapter 14: Under New Management.

Worship and Evangelizing

Simply Jesus. Chapter 8: Stories that Explain and a Message That Transforms.

Communities as sign of God's design

Udemy, Philippians (video), Section 2, Lecture 11 - https://www.udemy.com/paul-and-his-letter-to-the-philippians/learn/v4/t/lecture/3852978

Art opens our eyes

Surprised by Scripture. Chapter 11: Apocalypse and the Beauty of God

Justice implements the work of Christ
Creation, Power, Truth. Chapter 2: The New Imperialism.

Reminding the powerful
Creation, Power, Truth. Chapter 3: Spirit of Truth: the Witness of John.

Part FOUR. Living in God's new world

Four echoes in our souls
How are we lead through life?
Creation, Power, Truth. Introduction.

Longing for justice
Simply Christian. Chapter 1: Putting the World to Rights.

Enjoying beauty
Simply Christian. Chapter 2: For the Beauty of the Earth.

Graving connection
Simply Christian. Chapter 3: Made for Each Other.

Searching for meaning
Simply Christian: Chapter 2: The Hidden Spring.

Heaven and earth will marry
Three options how God relates to us
Simply Christian. Chapter 5: God.

Interlocking of heaven and earth
The Case for the Psalms. Chapter 5: All the Trees of the Forrest Sing for Joy.

How the movie ends
Surprised by Hope. Chapter 6: What the Whole World is Waiting For.

This is life after death: the dead will rise, and the earth will be as intended
Confused views on hope
Surprised by Hope. Chapter 1: All Dressed Up and No Place to Go.

Life after life after death
Surprised by Hope. Chapter 3: The Surprising Character of Early Christian Hope.

Like a trailer of the future
Simply Good News. Chapter 2: The Return of the One God.

What we did was not in vain
Deeds will last into the future
Surprised by Hope. Chapter 12: Rethinking Salvation.

What we do is not wasted
Simply Jesus. Chapter 15: Jesus, Ruler of the World.

Jesus rearranges everything
The Work of the People (video): Look at Jesus - http://www.theworkofthepeople.com/look-at-jesus

Outro: Which song do you sing?
Simply Jesus. Chapter 1: The Challenge to the Churches.

Footnotes :

[1] N.T. Wright, *Romans in a Week*, (Lecture Series 1992 at Regent College), https://www.regentaudio.com/products/romans-in-a-week
[2] Jesus Army, Talking to Tom Wright, http://jesus.org.uk/blog/talking-to/talking-to-tom-wright-part-1.
[3] *Christianity Today*, Surprised by NT Wright, http://www.christianitytoday.com/ct/2014/april/surprised-by-n-t-wright.html.
[4] *Time*, Should We Bring Heaven down to Earth? http://ideas.time.com/2012/04/05/should-we-bring-heaven-down-to-earth/.
[5] *The Work of the People*, Called to Study and Teach, http://www.theworkofthepeople.com/called-to-study-and-teach.
[6] N.T. Wright, *Scripture and the Authority of God: How to Read the Bible Today*, (New York: HarperCollins, 2011), 24.

[7] N.T. Wright, *The Case for the Psalms: Why They are Essential*, (New York: HarperOne, 2013), 52.
[8] *The Work of the People*, The Fulfillment, http://www.theworkofthepeople.com/the-fulfillment.
[9] N.T. Wright, *Surprised by Scripture: Engaging Contemporary Issues*, (New York: HarperOne, 2014), 60.
[10] N.T. Wright, *Simply Jesus: A New Vision of Who He Was, What He Did, and Why He Matters*, (New York: HarperCollins, 2011), 141.
[11] N.T. Wright, *Paul and Faithfulness of God. 2 vols. Christian Origins and the Question of God 4*, (Minneapolis: Fortress, 2013), 1043–44.
[12] N.T. Wright, *Simply Good News: Why the Gospel Is News and What Makes It Good,* (New York: HarperOne, 2015), 4.
[13] Wright, *Surprised by Scripture*, 6.
[14] N.T. Wright, *How God became King: The Forgotten Story of the Gospels*, (New York: HarperOne, 2012), 34–36.
[15] Ibid., 87.
[16] Ibid., 94.
[17] N.T. Wright, *Surprised by Hope: Rethinking Heaven, the Resurrection, and the Mission of the Church*, (New York: HarperOne, 2008), 56.
[18] N.T. Wright, *How Can The Bible Be Authoritative?* (The Laing Lecture 1989, and the Griffith Thomas Lecture 1989. Originally published in Vox Evangelica, 1991, 21, 7–32), http://ntwrightpage.com/Wright_Bible_Authoritative.htm.
[19] John 1:1
[20] John 1:14
[21] N.T. Wright, *Creation, Power and Truth: The Gospel in a World of Cultural Confusion,* (London: SPCK, 2013), 86.
[22] N.T. Wright, *Following Jesus: Biblical Reflections on Discipleship*, (Grand Rapids: Eerdmans, 1994), 35.
[23] An Angled mirror, behold the man (based on the lecture "Called to be Human: Agenda for Tomorrow's Church," November 2010, Trinity Western University, http://intothedesertblog.blogspot.de/2011/09/angled-mirror.html); see also N.T. Wright, Following Jesus, 35–39.
[24] Wright, How God became King, 239.
[25] Wright, Surprised by Scripture, 59.
[26] Wright, Simply Good News, 54.
[27] Wright, Surprised by Scripture, 94.
[28] Ibid., 32.
[29] Mark 1:15–16.

[30] *Jesus Army*, Talking to Tom Wright, http://jesus.org.uk/blog/talking-to/talking-to-tom-wright-part-1.
[31] N.T. Wright, *After You Believe: Why Christian Character Matters*, (New York: HarperOne, 2010), 36.
[32] Ibid., 70
[33] Wright, Simply Jesus, 212.
[34] Wright, Surprised by Scripture, 35.
[35] Wright, After You Believe, 243.
[36] Ibid., 157.
[37] *Udemy*, Worldviews, the Bible and the Believer, NT Wright, Professor, https://www.udemy.com/worldviews-the-bible-and-the-believer/learn/.
[38] *The Work of the People*, Crucified with Christ, minute 1, http://www.theworkofthepeople.com/crucified-with-christ.
[39] *Udemy*, Philippians, Q&A video, min 2.30.
[40] *Udemy*, Paul and His Letter to the Philippians, by NT Wright, Professor (overview, min 14.30), https://www.udemy.com/paul-and-his-letter-to-the-philippians/learn/.
[41] Wright, Surprised by Scripture, 6.
[42] Wright, Simply Jesus, 140.
[43] Wright, Surprised by Scripture, 61.
[44] Wright, Surprised by Hope, 69.
[45] Wright, Creation, Power and Truth, 18.
[46] Wright, Simply Good News, 27.
[47] Ibid., 65.
[48] Mike Breen, *Building a Discipleship Culture*, (3DM Publishing, 2014)
[49] Wright, Simply Good News, 56.
[50] Wright, Surprised by Hope, 293.
[51] Wright, Simply Jesus, 217.
[52] Wright, Simply Good News, 14.
[53] *Udemy*, Paul and his letter to the Galatians, by NT Wright, Professor, https://www.udemy.com/paul-and-his-letter-to-the-galatians/.
[54] Wright, Paul and Faithfulness of God, 404.
[55] N.T. Wright, *Evil and the Justice of God*, (Downers Grove, IL: InterVarsity, 2006), 125.
[56] Ibid., 126.
[57] Wright, Simply Jesus, 219.
[58] Wright, Creation, Power and Truth, 47.
[59] Wright, Evil and the Justice of God, 122.
[60] Wright, Surprised by Scripture, 178.

[61] Ibid., 177.
[62] Ibid., 178.
[63] Ibid., 193.
[64] Ibid., 193.
[65] Wright, Creation, Power and Truth, 9.
[66] N.T. Wright, *Simply Christian: Why Christianity Makes Sense*, (San Francisco: Harper, 2006), 49.
[67] Ibid., 26.
[68] Ibid., 58.
[69] Ibid., 115
[70] Wright, The Case for the Psalms, 22.
[71] Wright, Simply Good News, 34.
[72] Wright, Surprised by Hope, 19.
[73] Wright, Scripture and the Authority of God, 191.
[74] Wright, Paul and the Faithfulness of God, 548.
[75] Wright, How God became King, 44.
[76] Wright, Surprised by Hope, 41.
[77] Psalm 96:11–13.
[78] Psalm 98:7–8.
[79] Wright, Paul and Faithfulness of God, 1089.
[80] Wright, Surprised by Hope, 193.
[81] Ibid., 162.
[82] Ibid., 208.
[83] Ibid., 207.
[84] Wright, Simply Jesus, 211.
[85] *The Work of the People*, Look at Jesus, http://www.theworkofthepeople.com/look-at-jesus.
[86] Wright, Surprised by Scripture, 58.
[87] Wright, Simply Jesus, 5.
[88] Ibid., 5.

63157650R00080

Made in the USA
Charleston, SC
26 October 2016